482-7688

Vatican II] how priest used
changes] to face

Vatican
Council II The
Conciliar
Post Conciliar Documents

Church, Sacraments and Ministry

The Wrath of the Lamb
The Pioneer Ministry
Beyond Anglicanism
Jesus Christ in the Old Testament
Studies in Pastoral Epistles
Studies in Paul's Technique and Theology
Grace and Truth
The Pastoral Letters
St Paul's Understanding of Jesus
Teilhard Reassessed (Ed)
Vindications (Ed)
Book of Job (with Miriam Hanson)
Revelation of St John the Divine (with Ronald H. Preston)

MOWBRAYS LIBRARY OF THEOLOGY

Church, Sacraments and Ministry

Anthony Hanson
Professor of Theology, University of Hull

Series Editor: Michael Perry

MOWBRAYS LONDON & OXFORD

© *Anthony Hanson 1975*

First Published 1975
by A. R. Mowbray & Co. Ltd.
The Alden Press, Osney Mead
Oxford OX2 0EG

ISBN 0 264 66255 5

Printed in Great Britain
at the Alden Press, Oxford

Introduction to Mowbrays Library of Theology

The last quarter of the twentieth century is a good time for the Christian Church to take stock of its beliefs. In the course of the century, Christian theology has had many challenges to meet—and has itself not remained unchanged by the encounter. Society has become more pluralist and less committed; dogmatism is at a discount. Christianity has had to survive in a climate which regards its beliefs as matters of opinion rather than of fact, and in a world not readily convinced of their relevance either to public politics or private morals. Within the faith (and particularly in the sixties of the century) there have been radical questionings of almost every aspect of doctrine.

Despite all this, there are signs that people are more willing now than they were a decade or so ago to listen to more constructive voices. Christians need to state how they can—as men of their own age and culture, and as heirs to the radical ferment of ideas which characterised the mid-century—articulate a faith in God, Father, Son and Holy Spirit, hold convictions about the nature of man and his destiny, and show the relevance of belief to conduct. The contributors to this series think it their duty to give as plain and straightforward a statement as is compatible with their intellectual integrity of what the Christian faith is, and how it can be honestly and meaningfully expressed today.

Christian faith has always been the faith of a community. It is therefore necessary to 'earth' such an articulation in terms of a particular community of Christians. So the contributors to this series are all Anglicans, confident that theirs is a particular expression of the universal faith which still merits serious consideration. The series therefore aims to reflect, not only themes of interest to all Christians at all times, but also particular aspects of Christian theology which are currently exercising the Church of England in congregations and Synods. And, since there will always be rival religions and ideologies competing for men's allegiance, we need to explore their claims and ask what the attitude of Anglicans is towards them. But that the Church has a faith which is worth stating and that it is a faith to live by, is a convinction shared by every contributor.

Michael Perry

Contents

Acknowledgements

I wish to express my gratitude to the Ven. Michael Perry Archdeacon of Durham, for his advice and guidance in planning this book and also to my wife for undertaking at short notice the task of proof reading and to my son Philip for help in compiling the Indexes.

Univ. of Hull, June 1975. *A.T. Hanson*

Abbreviations used: BCP: Book of Common Prayer. CSI: Church of South India. NEB: New English Bible. RSV: Revised Standard Version.

To all my colleagues in the Andra United Theological College and in Dornakal Diocese, who taught me more about the nature of the Church than I could have learned from any amount of reading.

A.T. Hanson

1   The Church in history

AT a time like the present, it may seem irrelevant or even
irresponsible on the part of a professional theologian to discuss
so apparently secondary a topic as the theology of the Church,
of the sacraments, and of the ordained ministry. The very
foundations of the Christian faith are being called into
question by many educated people; moreover the Christian
Church in the West is on the defensive, is declining in
numbers, and is exercising less influence in society than it has
for many centuries. But the Church has not disappeared in the
West; on the contrary it is experiencing in some respects an
intellectual renewal. Christianity is being re-examined with a
new interest in some circles where this might least have been
expected. As long therefore as the Church exists, it will be
necessary to give some intelligible account of what it is and
what it ought to be; and this is in fact the same thing as
attempting to work out a theology of the Church. Moreover
history shows that at least the two great sacraments of the
gospel are the means by which the Church has built up and
nourished its life from age to age; and indeed, as we shall be
seeing, the sacrament of the eucharist is at the moment
enjoying something like a revival and re-orientation
throughout the Christian Church in most traditions. Add to
this the fact that there is probably more original thinking going
on today about the nature of the Church's ministry than has
been the case since the Reformation, and I do not think that we
need make any further apology for writing a book on Church,
sacraments, and ministry.

On the other side, we may encounter the objection that
clergy and laity of the Church of England do not need to
trouble their heads about the theology of the Church, the

sacraments, or the ministry. Most of them, it might be argued, are able to get along quite well without very much theology; problems connected with these areas of Christian life can be solved by common sense and a willingness to compromise as each of them crops up. This is a short-sighted view; most of the problems we encounter today in this area have their roots in theology. How, for example, can you seriously negotiate with other Christians if you are very vague as to what you believe about the nature of the Church? Or how can we revise our eucharistic liturgy with any hope of success if we have no idea of what we mean by the eucharist? How can we face the fierce criticism about current baptismal practice in our Church that is being directed at us from inside the Church itself unless we are prepared to think afresh about the significance of baptism? How are we to deploy our clergy and laity so as best to meet the demands of a rapidly changing social situation if we are unwilling to study the nature and purpose of the ordained ministry? A non-commital attitude towards theology may be well enough in a period of stability and generally accepted orthodoxy. But in a time like the present, when everything is being challenged, it is disastrous. We must be prepared to think out our beliefs, or we will find that we have unintentionally lost them.

We begin, then, with the theology of the Church as we find it in the New Testament. Old-fashioned theologians, influenced by passages such as Matt. 16.16f. (the promise to Peter); 18.15f. (disputes to be heard before the Church); and John 17.20 (the prayer for future believers), tended to represent our Lord as deliberately planning the organisation of a Church which he knew would have to endure throughout many centuries of turbulent history. This is a misleading picture. We must not attribute to the historical Jesus a superhuman knowledge of future history. But, perhaps by reaction from this view, some scholars, following the lead of the great Albert Schweitzer, have concluded that Jesus could not possibly have envisaged the existence of anything like a continuing Church, since he was expecting that the end of the world would take place almost immediately after his own death. It would follow that all apparent references to the Church or community of disciples which are attributed to him in the gospels are creations of the early Christian community. But this view is no more probable than the old-fashioned one.

We must not, it is true, speak of Jesus as 'founding' the Church in the same way in which, for example, Baden Powell founded the Scout Movement. We have no proper evidence to suggest that Jesus planned the structure of the Church, or indeed that he intended to 'found' a new religion. One may say of the founders of all the great world religions, in so far as these religions had founders, that they did not set out initially to begin a new religion. This is as true of Gautama Sakyamuni and of Mohammed as it is of Jesus. But there are certain indications in Jesus' teaching and certain implications in his claims that do point to his awareness of a community orientated round himself.

Much of Jesus' language implies the existence of a group of disciples who are the recipients and heirs of his teaching, though it is often the case that their response to what he asks of them is inadequate. We think of Luke 12.32: 'Fear not, little flock'; compare with this Mark 14.27, the citation from Zechariah about the shepherd and his flock, a text also used by the Qumran community about their leader and his group of followers. We think also of the figure of the bridegroom and of the wedding feast which occurs so often in Jesus' teaching. If you ask 'Who is the bride?', the answer can only be 'the Church'. The guests must also be regarded as part of the community. Here also comes the account of the institution of the eucharist, which presupposes a group to observe it. Indeed Mark 14.25 suggests that this is an anticipation of the messianic banquet.

The appointment of the Twelve also implies the nucleus of a community. Why *twelve*, except that in some sense they represented the twelve tribes of the renewed Israel? There are two passages in the first Gospel, Matt. 16.16f. and 18.17f. where the word 'Church' (*ekklēsia*) is directly attributed to Jesus. Of these the latter has all the marks of a later construction, but the first cannot be so easily dismissed. It is perhaps the most controversial passage in the entire Bible, since it forms the foundation stone for what the Roman

Catholic Church believes about the papacy:

> And I tell you, you are Peter, and on this rock I will build
> my church, and the powers of death shall not prevail against
> it. I will give you the keys of the kingdom of heaven, and
> whatever you bind on earth shall be bound in heaven, and
> whatever you loose on earth shall be loosed in heaven.

It is no doubt anachronistic to suggest that Jesus ever used any
word corresponding to 'Church' (whether the Aramaic
equivalent of the Hebrew *qāhāl* or some other word); but the
claim that discipleship of Jesus is based on faith in his
vocation is not anachronistic, and points towards a conception
of discipleship that implies the existence of the Church. If
however we speak (as we may) of the Church as being included
in Jesus' thinking, we must realise that that Church is nothing
if not an eschatological community; that is a community based
on the fact that in some sense the last days have arrived and
the rule of God is manifested in history. Where we find a
doctrine of the Church that completely omits the
eschatological element, we may be sure that it is not faithful to
the witness of the New Testament.

When we turn to the epistles, we find that the Church is
basically the people of God. There are numerous figures used
for the Church in the New Testament (Paul Minear, the
American scholar, distinguishes over ninety of them)[1], but we
shall never get this bewildering variety of figures into focus
unless at the outset we understand the Church as the people of
God. Moreover, unlike all the other figures, this is not a
metaphor. The New Testament writers claim that Christians
are quite literally God's people in the new age (the actual
phrase is used in 1 Pet. 2.10). All New Testament theology is
based on the assumption that the new Jewish–Gentile Church
has inherited the promises, duties, and privileges of Israel of
old. This is just as basic to Paul's thought as to that of any
other writer of the New Testament. For proof of this you have
only to turn to the long section in the Epistle to the Romans
consisting of chapters 9–11 in which Paul deploys all his
resources of learning and exegesis in order to prove that the
mixed Jewish–Gentile Church of his day has taken the place in

God's eyes of the old Israel. Again in a passage such as 1 Cor. 10.1–11 the comparison there drawn with the experiences of Israel of old in the wilderness would have no point at all if Paul did not regard Christians as the modern Israel. The very term so freely used by Paul for the Church, *ekklēsia*, is taken from the Septuagint translation of the Hebrew *qāhāl*, which is one of the two words used in the Hebrew Bible to denote the congregation of Israel. This is so much the case that Stephen in his speech in Acts 7.38 can refer to Israel of old as 'the *ekklēsia* in the wilderness' without in any way abating the Christians' claim to be the *ekklēsia* in his day. This claim perhaps meets us in its most emphatic form when we read in Rev. 2.9 and 3.9 of a certain group in Ephesus and in Philadelphia 'who say that they are Jews and are not'. This does not mean that there was a group of Gentiles in those cities masquerading as Jews. It refers in fact to the local synagogue in each of these cities and claims that they have lost their right to be called Jews. Christians are the true Jews.

The concept of the Church as the people of God has certain implications which have too often been forgotten in the history of the Church. In the first place, they are the people of God still in the wilderness. They have not yet entered the promised land. They are therefore not a settled, static, established body. They are still on the move; a pilgrim group. Then again, they are a *people*, *plebs sancta Dei*, the holy people of God as the Canon of the Latin Mass so finely calls them. They are not therefore essentially an army, or a nation, or a caste, or a club, nor even a republic or an autocracy. These are all misunderstandings of the nature of the Church into which Christians have fallen at some epoch or in some area. Thirdly, they should never forget that they are in some sense continuous with Israel of old, and therefore possess an inalienable relation with Israel after the flesh; that is with the Jewish people of today. That relation has been for most of the Church's history the disgraceful relation of persecutor to persecuted, but the Church has never quite been able to forget the relationship, and today more than ever Christians owe it to modern Judaism that they acknowledge Jews as at the very least their cousins in the faith and that they explore with penitence and sensitivity what should be the relation of Church to Synagogue in a post-Christendom era.

The understanding of the Church as the people of God can also appear as a liberating and ennobling ideal to non-Christians approaching the faith for the first time. I know from my own experience that outcastes among the Telugu people of South India who had recently joined the Church found great joy in the new lineage which Christianity gave them. After being a group without historical traditions or self-respect for centuries, they found themselves now possessing a new identity, and rejoiced to name Abraham as their forefather and the apostles as their brothers in Christ. Paul offers exactly the same privilege when he writes to his Gentile converts in Corinth: '*our* fathers were all under the cloud, and all passed through the sea' (1 Cor. 10.1).

There is one figure for the Church which stands out from all others in the New Testament: the figure of the Church as the body of Christ. It is confined almost exclusively to Paul's writings or those of his immediate disciples in Colossians and Ephesians (it appears to be implicit in the thought behind John 2.21, but nowhere else outside Paul). This figure has occupied a disproportionate place in theological thinking because it seems to link the theology of the Church so closely to Christology and even to metaphysics.

It is not an easy concept to understand; this is partly because Paul uses that word *sōma* (body) in so many different senses. He describes the Church as 'the *sōma* of Christ' in Rom. 12.5; 1 Cor. 12.13; Col. 1.18; 2.19; Eph. 1.23; 4.4 (but the usage in Colossians and Ephesians is not the same as in Roman and Corinthians; in the two later epistles Christ is the head of the Church which is the rest of the body; in the two former the Church is seen as the whole body of Christ). Paul also uses *sōma* of Christ and of Christians in a eucharistic context (1 Cor. 10.16–17; 11.24,27,29). Not content with that, he also uses *sōma* of Christ's risen body and of the body which Christians may hope to have at their resurrection (1 Cor. 15.35–44; 2 Cor. 5.6–10; Phil. 3.21). He can also use *sōma* to indicate man as a whole personality, either a regenerated personality, or one still under the dominion of the law (Rom. 7.24; 8.10; 12.1; 1 Cor. 6.18–19; Phil. 1.20).

In order to pick our way through this perplexing variety of usages, we cannot do better than follow the lead of E. Schweizer (not the famous Albert, but like him a distinguished Swiss scholar).[2] Paul's use of *sōma*, he says, is much more Hebrew than Greek, in the sense that for him *sōma* is not one part of man, but man looked at as a whole. Thus 'This is my body' means 'this is myself.' It follows that man can never be without a *sōma* except in the most exceptional and unwelcome circumstances. In Rom. 8.23, for example, 'the redemption of our bodies' does not mean our 'shuffling off this mortal coil'. Christ took a human body, which means he accepted human personality with all its characteristics. His life in that body (living, dying, rising again) must be manifested in the bodies (living human personalities) of Christians (2 Cor. 4.7–14). The connection between Christ and the believer is as close as is the connection between the two partners in the sexual act. This act ideally involves the giving of the whole personality by means of the physical body (see 1 Cor. 6.15–20). Redemption therefore means, not freeing the soul from a death-destined body, but bringing the body (personality) into obedience to, and unity with, God. In Paul *sōma* means the whole personality; it is therefore the sphere in which men serve God.

In the context of the eucharist Paul's emphasis is on 'my body which is for you'. 'Body' here does not mean a substance, or the principle of corporality, but 'personality given', just as the blood means 'life given'. The Lord gave himself for us, so he who receives the eucharist while insulting or ignoring his brother insults and ignores the Lord. The eucharist makes present to the Church that personality (Jesus Christ) given on its behalf; consequently that personality (the body of Christ) is the place where the Church is to be found. From this, says Schweizer, stems the use of 'body of Christ' in connection with the Church. In secular literature *sōma* could mean 'a collection or collectivity of individuals'. But Paul only uses *sōma* in this sense for the community, not for the individual. The individuals exist in the *sōma* but it cannot be said of any one individual that he is the *sōma*. The Church is dependent on Christ but Christ is not dependent on the Church. Schweizer writes: 'The crucified and risen Christ is for Paul a

contemporary sphere into which the Church is introduced.'
The Church thus becomes a unity; one body.

Some scholars and theologians have maintained that the use
of this figure by Paul implies that it is not in fact a figure at all,
but to be taken literally. The Church is identical with the body
of Christ. Michael Ramsey, till recently Archbishop of
Canterbury, has put it clearly: 'to call the Church "the body of
Christ" was to draw attention to it not primarily as a
collection of men, but as Christ himself in his own being and
life'.[3] Now it is quite true that Paul when he writes about the
body of Christ in this context means the risen body; what he
calls 'the spiritual body'. But this does not mean that the
Church and the body of Christ are so far identical as to be
interchangeable terms. Paul Minear well points out that when,
in 1 Cor. 15.14, Paul appeals to the fact of the risen Christ as
the justification for the Christian life, he does not appeal to the
fact of the Church: 'if Christ has not been raised, then our
preaching is in vain and your faith is in vain'. We must not
therefore treat the body-of-Christ figure as anything more than
a figure, though a profound and significant one. The Church is
not to be regarded as identical with the risen Christ. Paul's
thought, like that of almost every writer in the New Testament,
is eschatological. Christ's risen body, his 'spiritual body', is the
area prepared by God for the Church to occupy. The Church
can only now be called his body in so far as it is filled by the
Spirit, who is himself an anticipation of the *parousia* ('second
coming'). Only at the *parousia* will it be possible to say that
the Church is the body of Christ completely.

It is by means of this question of the *parousia* that we can
best perhaps understand why Paul worked out his doctrine of
the Church as the body of Christ. Any theologian who
seriously accepts the doctrine of the incarnation of God in
Christ must face one difficult question: after the resurrection of
Christ, what happened to his body? This is not the elementary
question about whether the tomb was empty or not. It is the
much profound question as to what happened to the human
personality Jesus Christ. That by the resurrection he showed
himself to be living and united with God, all Christians must
believe or cease to be Christians. But how is he related to us, to

believers? Paul answers this question in terms of Christ's spiritual body, using language which may seem strange and even meaningless at times to us, but which had a definite purpose when he used it, and can be understood in a meaningful sense by us in so far as we are faced with the same question. Christ, said Paul, exists now in the dimension of Spirit and is therefore the means whereby we, who are what he has been, human personalities existing in space–time, can ultimately enter upon the same experience of obedient life, death, and resurrection as he underwent.

Of course Paul expected the *parousia* very soon. He believed that our 'spiritual bodies' were waiting for us, speaking in terms of time, round the corner. We cannot believe that today. If the *parousia* did not take place when Paul thought it would, we have no reason to believe that it is imminent for us in a way which it has proved not to be for Paul. But in fact the Church, while never openly admitting that it was not expecting the *parousia*, has adapted itself to the realisation that it is not imminent. And for the expectation of the imminent *parousia* we can and should substitute the communion of saints. We can enter into the consciousness of sharing the same communion with Christians of all ages. We can join our prayers with theirs; in the eucharist we can be aware of worshipping with them. We can look forward at death to an experience of continuing life with them in God's presence mediated through the risen Christ. It is in this sense that we can speak of 'the mystical body of Christ', meaning the Church of those who have been redeemed and are being redeemed throughout the ages. We use the word 'mystical' not in order to avoid clear intellectual definition, but to indicate an experience which, though it must transcend our understanding, is not beyond our imagination and can be in some real sense enjoyed here and now.

We must make one more important point about the Church before leaving the Scriptures. It concerns a remarkable difference between two great theological traditions within the pages of the New Testament itself, the Pauline and the Johannine. Paul certainly holds a very high doctrine of the Church. But he never suggests that membership of the Church guarantees salvation. He is constantly warning his converts against relapsing and obviously believes that those who are baptised can be lost eternally. See 1 Cor. 10.1–11; and also 11.27–34, where Paul concludes that some Christians have died (and therefore presumably are lost) because of misbehaviour at the eucharist. See also 1 Cor. 9.27 and Phil. 3.12, where he envisages the possibility of himself proving to be 'disqualified'. At the beginning of 1 Corinthians he addresses his readers as 'the Church of God which is at Corinth, . . . those sanctified in Christ Jesus, called to be saints'; but goes on in the course of the epistle to accuse some of them of the grossest sins. Plainly Paul believed in a mixed Church, whose members were still on pilgrimage, any one of whom might while still in this life fall from grace and perish eternally.

Not so John. If we examine the Johannine literature carefully we shall find that serious sinners and apostates are regarded as never having really been part of Christ's flock. Since John wrote a gospel, it is not very easy to read off from it his doctrine of the Church. But this can be done if we consider the case of Judas Iscariot. In John 6.71 we learn that Jesus has chosen the Twelve but knows that one of them belongs to the enemy. In 13.10–18 the theme is amplified; Jesus knew who was destined to betray him; he knew that one had never been, and never would be, clean. In verse 18 we learn the reason: it was actually foretold in Scripture that one of the intimates of the Messiah should betray him. Last of all in 17.12 Judas is called 'the son of perdition'. One might argue that this doctrine applies to Judas only and cannot be generalised; but in the Fourth Gospel the Twelve seem to represent the Church. It looks therefore as if you are either predestined as a Church member to salvation or to perdition. In any case this account of John's doctrine of the Church is confirmed by what we read in the First Epistle of John. In 1 John 2.18–19 the author of the epistle, referring to certain apostates who are apparently setting up a rival sect, says of them that, though they have left the Church, they never really belonged to the Church. If they had really belonged to it they would never have left it. In tune with this is his reference in 5.16–17 to a 'mortal' sin: 'There is a sin which is mortal; I do not say that one is to pray for that.' This sin is almost certainly apostasy. The logical implication of this language is a doctrine of a pure, and therefore invisible, Church, whose members have indefectible grace. On the whole it looks as if the third great theological tradition in the New Testament agrees on this question with John rather than Paul. See Heb. 6.4–6, where we learn that apostates cannot be restored; they are beyond hope.

Both doctrines of the Church, the Pauline and the Johannine, have persisted throughout the Church's history and will no doubt be with us until the *parousia*. Paul's is the more practical. The early Church soon found that it had to devise means for re-admitting penitent sinners, even penitent apostates. On the other hand the Johannine view always keeps cropping up, especially in times of corruption and decay. The two views can only be reconciled from the point of view of the end of history. In other words, if we may for a moment attempt to look at the entire history of the human race from God's point of view, we would say that the total number of the redeemed in heaven at the end of history will constitute the real Church, the Church triumphant. In that sense those who appeared to be members of the Church while on earth, but who in fact did not persevere in faith till the end, never really were members of the Church as it ultimately turns out to be. In this sense, John, Augustine, and Calvin are right. But it is dangerous and presumptuous to try to look at things from God's point of view as a permanent habit; ecclesiastics have too often claimed to be speaking for God and have fallen into the most appalling errors thereby. It is better therefore, when we are trying to achieve a working theology of the Church applicable to a Church still on pilgrimage, to follow Paul's lead and conclude that no apparent member of the Church is to be regarded as having lost his membership during his life (though membership may be qualified by excommunication), whereas on the other hand no member of the Church while on earth may be regarded as possessing an inalienable guarantee of ultimate salvation thereby.

The need to work out a theology of the Church only arose when schisms and heretics began to appear on something more than a very local scale. Thus it is not until the middle of the third century that we find Cyprian writing a work on the unity of the Church, under the pressure of the various schisms with which he was threatened. As might be expected from one who had been trained in law and was faced with the practical task of managing a number of dioceses, Cyprian takes the 'common-sense' view that the true Church is the visible, institutional Church as organised under him and his colleagues, and outside this Church there can be no sacraments and no hope of salvation.

The Johannine view is reflected among the Alexandrian theologians, who distinguished between the visible institutional Church and the ideal Church to which all the elect belong. But they were for the most part philosophers of the Middle-Platonic period and not busy administrators. Augustine was both; he was also a greater theologian than Cyprian. He accepts the institutional Church as being the body of Christ, a mixed community. But he also makes a distinction between the visible and the invisible Church. The invisible Church consists of the fixed number of the elect known only to God and some of them may be outside the visible Church. But what we have to reckon with on earth is the visible Church, and that Church (following Cyprian) he sees as united by the episcopate, but also by communion with the see of St Peter at Rome. He thus bequeathed to the Middle Ages in the West the concept of the Church as a visible organic whole.

The doctrine of papal supremacy was gradually elaborated during the Middle Ages, reaching a climax in the Bull *Unam Sanctam* of Boniface VIII in 1302, in which he declared that it was necessary to salvation for every human creature to be subject to the Roman Pontiff. A century later the position of the papacy had considerably weakened owing to the removal to Avignon and the subsequent Great Schism, so that the Council of Constance in 1414–18 was able, with the agreement of the Pope, to declare that a General Council is superior to the Pope. In the course of the fifteenth century the papacy recovered its position of supremacy, but the high tide of the conciliar movement remained as a precedent and a tradition capable of being appealed to in later ages. In the meantime the Eastern half of Christendom went its way, increasingly blockaded by Muslim conquest. When the schism between East and West formally began in 1054 there were, of course, mutual excommunications. But these were not regarded as irrevocable, and various efforts were made to heal the schism; always these efforts were unsuccessful. To this very day the Orthodox Churches as a whole have never pronounced an official verdict on other Christian bodies, and their practice in receiving converts from other Churches has varied. An Orthodox representative, writing in 1952, could say that the Greek Orthodox Church claims to be the one continuous Catholic Church. He added: 'the great majority of Christian people for one reason (Roman Catholicism) or another (Protestantism) have ceased to belong to the one Catholic Church.'[4] This is probably as near as we can come to learning the general opinion of the Orthodox Church even today.

The event of the Reformation required urgently that the Reformers should provide a theology of the Church. The obvious temptation was to appeal from the institutional Church to the 'real' Church, from the visible Church to the invisible. It is very much to the credit of both Luther and Calvin that they did not do so. Instead they formulated a new definition of the Church: the Church, they said, is where the gospel is purely preached and the sacraments rightly celebrated (that is, celebrated according to the gospel). This definition could claim the authority of St Paul, as we have seen above in our reference to 1 Cor. 11.27–34. Neither Luther nor Calvin denied entirely that the elements of the Church were to be found within the unreformed Church, though Calvin wrote in a most disparaging manner of such elements of a Church as can be found there. A modern Roman Catholic writer has made an interesting comparison between what Calvin says about the 'papal' Church and what the Vatican II Synod says about non-Roman Catholic Churches; he is able to show that on the whole Vatican II is the more charitable.[5] Calvin adopted Augustine's distinction between the visible and the invisible Church, just as he followed Augustine in his predestinarian doctrine.

Some of the radical Reformers, Anabaptists as they were

called (spiritual ancestors of modern Baptists, Mennonites, and Independents), tended to claim for themselves the heritage of the Church of true Christians, contrasted with the visible, institutional Church. And on the whole the 'evangelical' wing of Christendom has shown a preference for retaining this distinction in their ecclesiology. But it must be said that generally speaking evangelical Christendom today is much less prone to elaborate a theology of the Church which unchurches other Christians than the Catholic wing has shown itself to be.

The Roman Church reacted to the Reformation by closing its ranks round the papacy. Only the tendency on the part of Catholic monarchs in Europe to foster nationalist movements within the Church in their dominions counteracted this trend; and the French Revolution acted as a violent check on all such tendencies. Thus the Roman Catholic Church in 1870, finding itself increasingly deserted by state governments, and encountering a growingly hostile intellectual atmosphere, apparently committed itself at the First Vatican Council to a form of centralised autocracy subject to an infallible Pope. In these circumstances, Roman Catholic theologians had the greatest difficulty in making any formal distinction between pagans and Christians who were not Roman Catholics. Even the Orthodox Church, whose orders they recognised, could not be accepted as constituting a real Church at all.

The Church of England pursued its own path at the Reformation. It certainly claimed to be a Reformed Church, and Article XIX in the Thirty-Nine Articles contains an impeccably Reformed definition of the Church:

> The visible Church of Christ is a congregation of faithful men, in which the pure Word of God is preached, and the Sacraments be duly administered according to Christ's ordinance in all those things that are of necessity requisite to the same.

But the Article goes on to refer to the Churches of Jerusalem, Alexandria, Antioch, and Rome. And Article XXXIV declares that 'Every particular or national Church hath authority to ordain, change, and abolish ceremonies or rites of the Church ordained only by man's authority.' This reminds us that the

Church of England's ecclesiology allows a place for national Churches. Indeed that has always been a distinctive mark of Anglican ecclesiology since the Reformation. Anglican apologists in the sixteenth and seventeenth centuries constantly maintained that the Church of England was not a breakaway Church, like the Evangelical Church in Germany or the Reformed Church in France. It was the same continuous Catholic Church that had at the Reformation 'washed its face'. It followed from this that all Englishmen belonged to the Church of England by birthright; and, declared the spokesmen for the Church of England, all Englishmen ought to acknowledge this.

It became increasingly obvious during the seventeenth century that all Englishmen did not intend to acknowledge this. The majority did, but there was a significant minority on the right who still wanted the mass and the authority of the Pope, and a much more substantial minority on the left who wanted a Reformation organised on the continental model. By the year 1700 both minorities had more or less settled down into some sort of *modus vivendi* with the government; the Roman Catholics still liable to occasional persecution, the Protestant Dissenters suffering not persecution but political disability. No informed Anglican doubted that the Church of England was Protestant. A number of very well-informed Anglicans claimed that it was also Catholic.

For the next century the state continued to support the Church of England; but by the first half of the nineteenth century it became obvious to thinking men that this support could no longer be expected. Nonconformists were being admitted to Parliament. In 1829 Catholic Emancipation showed that Roman Catholics would soon receive the same privilege. It was plain that every Englishman was not any longer to be regarded as either a member of the Church of England or someone who had to struggle for exemption from membership. Moreover the French Revolution and the spread of Deistic beliefs among the educated class suggested a still more radical development: not every Englishman could be regarded as a Christian. What then were supporters of the Church of England to say about the Church? What or where was the Church to be found?

Among Anglicans one group of men understood the situation and believed they had the answer. The Tractarians, led by Newman, Keble, and Pusey, declared that what constituted the Church of England was not the support of the state, still less the event of the Reformation. It was that Church's possession of a hierarchy standing in the apostolic succession. The Church of England was the only legitimate Church in England because it could show its lineage of authority right back to the apostles passed down by the hands of bishops through the ages. This theory of the Church came to be known as the Branch Theory. You may see it represented in diagrammatic form on the north wall of the nave in the parish church at Helmsley in Yorkshire, a church built by a Tractarian vicar. Since the Church is constituted by apostolic succession, episcopacy, and valid orders, only the Roman Catholic Church, the Orthodox Church, and the Church of England are genuine branches of the Church. Even the Roman Catholic Church, though it possesses valid orders, has no right to be in England, since the Church of England represents the Catholic Church in England. When Pope Pius IX in the middle of the nineteenth century established a Roman Catholic hierarchy in England, Pusey described it as 'the Italian mission'.

This theory of the Church was held by many (though perhaps it would never have been true to say 'most') Anglicans until quite recently. We must therefore imagine the entire body of Christians throughout the world as having entered the twentieth century holding a number of doctrines about the Church, most of which were quite incompatible with each other, and many of which carried the corollary that very many contemporary Christians, who to outward appearances were enjoying a flourishing Church life, were not in the deepest sense true members of the Church. How all this has changed during the last fifty years, we must now consider.

2 A theology of the Church

WHAT brought about the change referred to in the last chapter was the impact of the Ecumenical Movement. There have always been thoughtful Christians who deplored the divisions within the Church; but only towards the end of the last century did this sentiment gather very much support among Christians as a whole. By that time many Christians had begun to realise that no Church in Europe (far less outside it) could hope to benefit indefinitely from state support or patronage. The time must come when Christianity would have to stand on its own feet and in every country the Church would become a body quite separate from, and in some places antagonistic to, the state. But a Church divided and warring internally is in no fit condition to encounter the modern nation-state with its ever-increasing power. Moreover, a powerful reinforcement to the movement towards unity came from the missionary work of the Church in Asia and Africa. In most areas in those countries the newly founded Churches were small and weak. It is not surprising that Indians or Chinese converted to Christianity failed to see the significance of divisions which originated in historical and social circumstances totally foreign to theirs; they and the missionaries who worked with them soon began to demand some positive action towards uniting the Churches. In addition Churches in Asia and Africa were not normally established or supported by the state. Once therefore they had passed beyond their infancy and were beginning to assert their identity as Churches distinct from the parent body, they were at once aware of their weak and exposed position and naturally looked for support to their fellow-Christians in their own countries.

The Ecumenical Movement began among non-Roman

Catholic Churches, and the first outstanding fruit of this movement came in 1947 in the shape of a union between Christians of different traditions. In South India a united Church was formed which included Anglicans, Methodists, Presbyterians, and Congregationalists. The union, which had been preceded by twenty-eight years of negotiations, was received with mixed feelings by many people in the Church of England. The difficult problem of recognition of non-episcopal ministries had been resolved by the Free Church elements in the new Church of South India consenting to accept episcopacy as the framework of ministerial order, while the Anglicans refrained from requiring that any of the existing ministers in the Free Churches entering the union should be episcopally ordained. From the moment of union all new ordinations were to be by the hands of the bishops. Thus non-episcopal orders would gradually disappear.

The union was loudly denounced by many Anglo-Catholics. The distinguished poet T. S. Eliot wrote a pamphlet in which he described it as 'a pantomime horse'. But twenty-seven years later it is possible to claim with confidence that the critics were wrong. The Church of South India has neither exhibited the features of a pan-Protestant amalgam nor has it fallen apart through attempting to reconcile inconsistent principles. It has grown in strength; episcopacy is highly valued and shows a more primitive and effective pattern than that of which the Church of England can boast. Its eucharistic liturgy is, historically speaking, more catholic than is the service of the Book of Common Prayer of 1662. It has been accepted into full communion with the Church of England. Its example has been followed (though not in the method of unifying the ministry) by an extensive union of Churches which produced the Church of North India in 1970. Other union schemes involving Anglicans are under active consideration in many parts of the world.

But such a movement towards union was bound to affect the doctrine of the Church held by Anglicans. It is increasingly difficult for any Anglican to hold the view that Free Church orders are null and void, if he wishes to retain any contact with reality. The Branch Theory of the Church begins to look less and less credible as more and more dioceses or provinces of the Anglican Communion dissolve into local united Churches. Above all it appears that Anglicanism and the Church traditions of the continental Churches of the Reformation, far from being mutually inconsistent, can co-exist in the same Church with mutual benefit. In other words, the Ecumenical Movement has put a question mark against many of the ecclesiologies of the Churches of the Reformation.

Until about 1950 it seemed that the Roman Catholic Church was immune from the ecumenical influence. It refused all invitations to ecumenical conferences and continued to treat all Christians outside its fold as schismatics and heretics whose only proper course is to return to the mother Church. But, as we now know, the leaven of ecumenism was working inside the Roman Church; when John XXIII came to the papal throne in 1958 it soon became apparent that there was to be a change. He called together the Second Vatican Council in 1962, and invited the non-Roman Catholic Churches to send observers to it. Though he died during the Council in 1963, the work continued under his successor Paul VI, and the Council, before it ended in 1965, produced two documents which materially altered the attitude of the Roman Catholic Church towards other Christians, and consequently altered in some significant degree its traditional doctrine of the Church.

The first document, known as *Lumen Gentium*, was about the nature of the Church. The old exclusive claims were here, so that it could be interpreted in a conservative sense; but there were also new accents heard, suggesting that even among Christians outside the Roman Church some elements of genuine Church life could be found. In the first place it describes non-Roman Catholic Churches as 'ecclesial communities'; it says of them 'in some real way they are joined with us in the Holy Spirit'. It says of the true Church that it 'subsists in the Catholic Church'; it does not merely identify the true Church with the Roman Catholic Church; and it adds that 'many elements of sanctification and truth can be found outside her visible structure'.

The other document, the *Decree on Ecumenism*, goes further; those at present born into separated communions must not be charged with the sin of separation:

> The Catholic Church Accepts them with respect and affection as brothers . . . men who believe in Christ and have been properly baptised are brought into a certain, though imperfect, communion with the Catholic Church. . . . some, even very many of the most significant elements and endowments which together go to build up and to give life to the Church herself can exist outside the visible boundaries of the Catholic Church.[1]

This is a new step forward. Never since the Reformation has the Roman Catholic Church recognised other (Reformed) Churches as existing in any sort of way. We should not object that the phrase 'ecclesial communions' is used of our Churches. In one sense the Church of Rome is quite right to insist that there can be only one Church. To use the phrase 'the Churches' of the denominations is, strictly speaking, nonsensical. We cannot of course agree that only the Church of Rome has the right to the title of 'the Catholic Church'. But we can be confident that the theologians of that Church are even now revising and renewing their ecclesiology; and we can admit that the renewal within the Church of Rome has drastically disorientated the Churches of the Reformation, and that this is to their great benefit. We too have been shaken out of traditional entrenched positions.

In our attempt, then, to work out a theology of the Church which will make sense in the present situation of Christianity, we begin by asking: who are the members of the Church? The overwhelming majority of Christians throughout the ages would answer this by saying: the members of the Church are those who have been baptised in the name of the Trinity. We do not need to repudiate this answer. On the contrary, baptism as the basis of membership of the Catholic Church is acquiring a renewed significance in view of the important place which it holds in the ecclesiology of the Roman Catholic Church ever since Vatican II. But this simple answer needs to be qualified in two directions. First, we may ask: is baptism all that is necessary for membership? We shall be considering this question in greater detail in our next chapter. So we may go on

to the second qualification: what about the members of
Christian denominations which do not practise baptism,
notably the Religious Society of Friends (Quakers) and the
Salvation Army? Are they not members of the Church? Of
course we must admit that they are. But we may note *en
passant* the interesting comment of Fr. Bernard Leeming on
these two bodies, that they look more like religious orders
within the whole Church than constituent parts of the Catholic
Church.[2] Both these bodies were perhaps originally intended to
be ginger-groups inside the Church rather than separate
denominations. There is another relevant consideration: it is
much easier to dispense with baptism in a Christendom
situation. Where most people are going to be baptised anyway,
the fact that a small minority of Christians are not baptised
does not make very much difference. Where the Church is
planted in a non-Christian environment baptism acquires
much greater significance. For example, in South India
baptism as the mark of the Christian is, even from a purely
sociological point of view, essential for the survival of the
Church. Without it, the Church would certainly have merged
into the circumambient and all-absorbing Hinduism (indeed
even with baptism this has happened once already in the
remote past in the Tamil Nad). There is even some evidence
that in those parts of the world where the Society of Friends
has undertaken missionary work in a pagan environment it has
not been averse to observing the two gospel sacraments. One
might almost formulate a law: where a Church finds itself the
only Church in a non-Christian milieu, it survives by means of
baptism and the eucharist. Thus we may reasonably claim that
Christian denominations which do not practise baptism can
only survive *in the long run* because all the other denomination
do practise it.

The visible Church consists of those who are baptised. This
may well seem a shocking claim in a country where there are
perhaps millions of people who have been baptised, but who
play virtually no part in the life of the Church; only attending
the Church's worship on the rarest occasions. Would it not be
better to define the Church's membership in terms of real
Christians, not nominal Christians? This is at first sight a most

attractive suggestion, but it encounters great difficulties. How do you know who are the real Christians? Any test you apply will seem to define Christianity in terms of what we do, or experience, rather than in terms of what God has done. If, for example, you say that real Christians are those who are really committed to Christ, or who have had an experience of conversion, you are in effect saying that we do not know who the real Christians are, because we cannot (indeed we should not) make absolute judgements as to how far someone is committed to Christ, or as to the quality of someone's conversion. But, as we have already observed, we cannot build a working ecclesiology on the basis of an invisible Church membership. This is not to deny, of course, that we need a doctrine of an invisible Church as well as of a visible one. Apart from anything else, the great majority of the Church consists of those who have departed this life and are with God in Christ. Moreover no thoughtful Christian would disagree with the statement that the final membership of the Church, the number of those who will remain faithful to the end, is known only to God. But in the meantime we need a working definition of the Church, and we cannot do better than begin with baptism as the foundation of Church-membership. But it is only the foundation. We must now consider what else is involved.

Theologians who discuss the nature of the Church usually arrange their discussion under the head of 'the Notes of the Church', and that is what we propose to do. There are traditionally four Notes of the Church, which are indicated by the four epithets applied to the Church in the Nicene Creed: 'one holy catholic and apostolic Church'. We begin then with the *unity* of the Church. The problem here is of course that there can be only one Church, yet it is perfectly obvious that, as constituted in the world today, the Church is divided into dozens of separate, and to some extent competing denominations. Even if we are willing to ignore institutional divisions and view the Church as consisting of various theological traditions, the dividedness is still glaring: we have the Roman Catholic, Orthodox, Lutheran, Baptist, Reformed, Anglican, and Methodist traditions, to name only some of the main ones. How are we to make sense of this? One way is to opt for one of the denominations and say that this is the true Church, while all other 'Churches' are illegitimate bodies masquerading as Churches. Until recently this was what Roman Catholics said in effect; and many Anglicans said this about non-episcopally ordered Churches. The objections to this are obvious: everyday experience suggests that Christian life, holiness and love is not confined to any one denomination. By any criteria available, the grace of the sacraments cannot honestly be said to be confined to any one denomination, nor to any combination of denominations, such as episcopally ordered Churches. The plain fact is that God has blessed all the denominations with his presence and grace, not in equal measure or at every point everywhere, but sufficiently so to make it monstrous and incredible to hold that any one denomination, or group of denominations, is regarded by him as more legitimate than the others.

Many Christians, freely admitting this, have gone to the other extreme. Christianity, they say, is based on the freedom of the human person; therefore a wide variety of forms of Christianity such as we enjoy today is intended by God and should be accepted by us. In other words, the Church is meant to exist in a number of denominations, each organised independently of the others. Let each Christian join the denomination which suits him best; let us drop all barriers to intercommunion, and also all attempts at organic union, and be content to remain as we are in fraternal concord. I think the best reply to this suggestion is to relate a conversation which I had some years ago in South India with an Indian colleague who served with me on the staff of the same seminary. He had been converted while a young man from Hinduism and became a Congregationalist, because that was the only form of Christianity that existed in the part of South India where he lived. But on union he had encountered the traditions of the other uniting Churches and had been particularly attracted by the liturgical tradition which was one of Anglicanism's contributions to the union. 'Why', he asked me, 'were we not told about this when we were Congregationalists?' In other words, he was protesting because Indians in his part of India had only been offered part of the Christian tradition. They had a right to enjoy the whole. As long as we remain organised in separate denominations, even if intercommunion prevailed everywhere, we are unable to share with other Christians the spiritual treasure God has given us, or to take advantage of theirs. When one listens to the way some Christians approach the very notion of organic union with other Christians, one gains the impression that denominational divisions were invented in order to prevent Christians from sharing their spiritual riches. In addition, the suggestion that we do not need organic union makes much better sense in the West than in the East. Western Christians may be able to afford the luxury of a full range of denominational choice, but this is not possible for the great majority of Christians in Africa and Asia. For them some sort of a united Church is the only hope of enjoying the full riches of Christianity.

We must therefore conclude that the Church is one, and that its unity ought to be shown clearly to the world. In the seventeenth chapter of John's Gospel Jesus on the eve of his passion prays 'that they all may be one, that the world may believe'. This was not an ineffective prayer: the unity of the Church was constituted by the cross and resurrection. But Christians by their denominational disunity have obscured the underlying real unity of the Church. There is a true parallel here with the calling of the individual Christian: each Christian is a 'saint' in the Pauline sense that he has been redeemed and is called to 'be what he is', that is to live a life worthy of what God has done for him. In so far as he does this he shows forth to the world that redemption which God has given him. So with the unity of the Church: it is one, and is called to show forth that unity to the world. We must not hesitate to draw the conclusion that our present divisions are wrong and that God wishes us to end them. This is not the same as saying that we are responsible for causing them, nor does it imply anything about how we should set about ending them. But it should be our goal to end the divisions of Christianity at least to the extent of enabling all Christians to share in the spiritual riches which we severally enjoy, and to manifest to the world the unity of the Church a great deal more effectively than is being done at present.

Secondly, the Church is *holy*. As with the statement that the Church is one, we are tempted to say that it obviously is not holy. It is made up of many people who fall short of the holiness which God demands. In some areas and in some epochs it seems to have forgotten altogether that it is not an ordinary human institution, part of the world. Consequently there is always a strong urge on the part of the more zealous Christians to break away from the existing Church and set up a pure, uncompromised Church. There may be circumstances in which this is justified (we think of the Confessing Church in Nazi Germany), but it is always a dangerous undertaking. If the sole criterion is holiness, who is to apply it? Christianity has always known 'holiness sects', and their natural history is quite familiar. Sooner or later someone in the sect begins to have doubts about the holiness of his fellow-members, and another breakaway occurs. After all, one can never be quite sure of the holiness of anyone else, and if one is sure of one's own holiness one is precisely in the position of the Pharisee in the parable and has become exactly the sort of person whom Jesus most specifically condemned. So, though enthusiasts and 'freak' Christians do from time to time break away and form their own groups of 'pure' Christians, these groups always exhibit a fissiparous tendency; or else they develop in a generation or so into just one more ordinary denomination.

Catholic Christians tend to believe that, though individual Christians are often very far from attaining the holiness to which they are called, the total Church is pure, holy, and even infallible. This could be wishful thinking: in compensation for the obvious sinfulness of the empirical Church one invents a projection in the form of an ideal Church and claims that that at least is holy. Perhaps one's belief in the absolute holiness of the Church depends on how literally one takes the figure of the Church as the body of Christ. We do after all say in the Creed 'I believe in one holy catholic and apostolic Church'. One should believe in the Church in the full sense of the words; the Church has a claim on the loyalty of Christians, and in this Catholics set a fine example to Protestants. The infallibility of the Church is another question; for Roman Catholics it is

closely bound up with the infallibility of the Pope, a question
which we do not propose to consider here. If you believe that
the Church as a whole is infallible, you are under some
obligation to say how its infallibility finds expression. If there
are no tests whereby we can know when the infallible authority
is speaking infallibly, its infallibility is useless. Perhaps most
Anglicans at any rate would prefer to follow the example of a
recent Roman Catholic scholar, Hans Küng, and speak rather
of the indefectibility of the Church.[3] God will not permit the
Church as a whole to go disastrously wrong. He will not allow
the Gospel and the Christian life to disappear from history.

Thirdly, the Church is *catholic*. The word itself only means
'universal', but traditionally the epithet has carried all sorts of
overtones. Especially since the Reformation, 'catholic' has
been appropriated by the Roman Catholic Church, and most
Protestants will say quite happily 'we are not Catholics', a
statement which in the early centuries would have been
tantamount to an admission of heresy and schism. Certainly
one can distinguish some characteristics of the Church in
history which are closely associated with the catholic
tradition: episcopacy, fixed liturgy, religious orders, auricular
confession, centrality of the eucharist in Sunday worship,
adoration of the reserved sacrament, fasting, observance of the
Church's year, cult of the saints, veneration of the Virgin
Mary, etc. Till recently all these have distinguished the
Catholic wing of Christianity as contrasted with the Protestant
wing, that is, the Roman Catholic Church, the Eastern
Orthodox Church, the Anglican Communion (for the most
part). The line is not clear-cut: Scandinavian Lutherans have
episcopacy, liturgy, and observe the Church's year, for
instance. The Orthodox do not practise adoration of the
reserved sacrament.

But the picture is changing before our eyes. In the first place,
Protestants are increasingly adopting Catholic practices.
Recently I met a Canadian Baptist woman missionary who,
because she had taught in a seminary largely patronised by the
Church of South India, was quite accustomed to celebrating a
Sunday eucharist according to the very catholic CSI rite; and
to whom episcopal oversight was neither unfamiliar nor

repugnant. Recently a Methodist minister in England published a book commending the use of the rosary.[4] More and more Christians whose Churches stem from the Reformation are becoming accustomed to frequent celebration of the eucharist; some even weekly. Liturgical worship is on the increase among Protestants. Episcopacy is no longer a bugbear to all Protestants. On the other hand the Roman Catholic Church is becoming more critical about some 'catholic' practices which have hitherto been sacrosanct, fasting communion for instance. Auricular confession is not now so rigorously insisted on; it is even possible that the cult of the saints and of the Blessed Virgin is in process of being modified and critically examined, though not, we may be sure, abandoned. In fact the catholicity of the Church is being more widely spread over the entire body of Christians, so that the Catholic–Protestant dividing line is being very much blurred. Anglicans, who have always maintained that the Church must be both Catholic and Reformed, should rejoice at this.

In German Lutheranism there is still an influential group of scholars who deplore what they call *Frühkatholikismus*, that is the appearance of 'catholic' elements very early in the life of the Church; such features as episcopal government, appeal to doctrinal tradition and orthodoxy, emphasis on the sacraments. Since these features can be traced within the New Testament itself (for example, in the Pastoral Epistles), such scholars are prepared to distinguish a canon within the canon and stand by that. They renounce those parts of the New Testament which exhibit 'catholic' elements. Hans Küng well remarks of the eminent scholar Ernst Käsemann, who has shown himself to be a stern critic of early Catholicism, that his protest against the catholicism of the Church has turned into a protest against the catholicism of Scripture.[5] For myself I believe that some of the most basic elements in catholicism (authorised ministry and the centrality of the eucharist, for example) are essential for the survival of the Church in history. The emergence of early Catholicism was not a symptom of decadence but of the determination of the Church to survive.

Fourthly, the Church is *apostolic*. Originally this meant that it could trace its teaching authority in a direct line right back to the apostles, as contrasted with heretical sects whose teaching originated with some more recent heresiarch. After this the meaning was modified by adding the claim that in the Catholic Church the succession of ordination could be traced unbroken back to the apostles. Both claims, when made by Church writers from the second century onward, were only relatively true. What the Fathers taught was more like what the apostles taught (as far as this can be recovered) than what the heretics taught. It was by no means identical. The claim to unbroken succession of ordination right back to the apostles fails at the most critical point, the period between the apostles and those who came after them (we shall be returning to this later).

Looked at from the standpoint of today, episcopal succession does have an impressive lineage, though it cannot be traced back to the apostles, so it is difficult to see in what sense it can be described as 'the apostolic ministry'. Behind this desire to trace one's tradition back to the apostles lies a perfectly legitimate desire to base the Church's authority on the very earliest tradition. It must be confessed that the authority of the Church presents one of the most intractable problems with which the modern Christian is faced. He can no longer say with old-fashioned Protestants 'the Bible only is the religion of Protestants'. The Bible needs interpreting, most of all today when we have to reckon with the critical approach. But the Catholic also finds the question much less simple than it seemed to be even as recently as ten years ago: 'My authority is the Pope' would have been his claim then. Today it is much more doubtful how far the Pope's authority is effective; how far he can command obedience on his word alone. But the Church at some times and on some subjects must exercise authority, and that authority must somehow be seen to be based on the original revelation in Jesus Christ. There must be some standards of faith; there must be some point at which it is possible to say: 'No, that version of Christianity is incompatible with the gospel'. At this precise epoch in history so many hitherto accepted authorities are being questioned that it is extraordinarily difficult to say wherein the authority of the Church consists and how it is to be exercised. We must content ourselves with two observations: (a) There are only three ultimate sources of authority for Christians: the Bible, the Church's tradition (or experience through the ages), and the Christian's own religious experience. Any attempt at imposing an authority that ignores one of these three is bound to fail. (b) We may legitimately hope that Catholics and Protestants together may try to work out a satisfactory method or methods by which authority can be rightly exercised in the Church.

There is also a sense of 'apostolic' which means 'missionary'. The Church is always called to be apostolic in the sense that it is called to proclaim the gospel. This meaning has come more to the fore recently as Christendom has decayed. Churches in non-Christian lands can teach Western Christians a great deal here. Certainly a Church that makes no effort to proclaim the gospel is gradually ceasing to be the Church. There are Churches that are in danger of just this. Churches which cater for only one class or community in society (for example the Armenian Church in India); Churches which identify themselves completely with one particular political programme (for example the Dutch Reformed Church in South Africa, and all major Churches in Northern Ireland). To such Christians the apostolicity of the Church should come as a rebuke and a challenge.

After this discussion of the nature of the Church, we must make some effort to decide what sort of a theology of the Church it is that we as Anglicans should accept. There never has been an official Anglican doctrine of the Church (it could legitimately be asked whether there ever has been an official Anglican doctrine of anything; Anglicanism is not a confessional body); but over the past hundred and fifty years the Branch Theory of the Church has been held in one form or another by a great many Anglicans, some of them very influential and eminent. Today, it must be admitted, this theory seems to be singularly out of touch with reality. Those who hold it must maintain, for example, that the Ethiopian Church is a genuine branch of the Church, while the Church of Scotland is not, because the Ethiopian Church has the apostolic succession and therefore valid orders, whereas the

Church of Scotland has not. But the Ethiopian Church is loaded with an accretion of centuries of superstition and illiteracy, so grotesquely unlike most other forms of the Church as to be hardly recognisable; while the Church of Scotland can show a standard of learning, preaching, and Christian living, combined with devout celebration of the sacraments, that compares favourably with the Church of England.

Or we must take another anomaly, this time from the continent of Europe. Where according to the Branch Theory of the Church, is the Catholic Church to be found in the Netherlands? We have here not only a Roman Catholic Church with full hierarchy and parish system, but also an Old Catholic Church (with orders recognised as valid by the Pope) side by side with it. Are there two Catholic Churches in Holland? Absurd! Is it the case then that somehow the Catholic Church in Holland has managed to duplicate itself? Or go a little farther north, and contemplate the Lutheran Church in Denmark. Here is a Church which does not qualify according to the Branch Theory, because tactual succession from the pre-Reformation episcopate was deliberately avoided at the time of the Reformation when the Reformed episcopate was being set up. Then cross the short sea frontier into Sweden, and you find a Church which is almost identical with that of Denmark in order, liturgy, and doctrine, but in the case of Sweden succession with the mediaeval episcopate was maintained. Does what was almost an historical accident make all the difference between being the Church and being an irregular conventicle of laymen? It is very hard to believe that it does.

The fundamental objection to the Branch Theory of the Church is that it makes the Church depend on the ministry, instead of *vice versa*. We shall be discussing this at greater length in our last chapter, but we might note that this external method of estimating the validity of the Church is characteristic of the Victorians, and the Victorian era was the heyday of the Branch Theory of the Church. Perhaps it was owing to the subtle influence of the contemporary theory of the physical universe, which regarded the ultimate unit of matter as a billiard-ball-like atom connected by purely external relations with all the other atoms in the universe, that induced Victorian churchmen to be so extraordinarily materialistic and even mechanistic in their beliefs about the Church. Many Anglican clergy apparently believed that, as long as your orders came down through a pipeline from the Apostles, it did not really matter whether that pipeline was integrated into the contemporary Church or not. Some of them even surreptitiously approached some disreputable *episcopus vagans* or other, who had (they believed) actually been ordained within the correct succession, in order to have their own orders corrected or emended. Once let your doctrine of the Church depend exclusively on your doctrine of the ministry, and you will find yourself ultimately led into absurdities such as these. We must therefore regard the Branch Theory of the Church as no longer credible.

We mentioned in a previous chapter that the notion of a national Church was congenial to Anglicanism. It was not peculiar to Anglicanism, because the concept of national Churches and their rights played some part in mediaeval ecclesiology, especially during the conciliar period. The idea has also played a part in Lutheran ecclesiology, since Luther was a champion of the rights of national Churches. But the Church of England began its career as a reformed Church on the assumption that a national Church had the right to order its own affairs independently of the Bishop of Rome, and Anglicans have ever since tended to think in terms of national Churches. In the course of the last two centuries the Anglican Communion has grown up all over the world into the form of a union of autonomous national Churches. In some parts of the world Anglicans have actually encouraged national Churches to establish themselves as catholic Churches independent of the Pope, as for example is the Lusitanian Church in Portugal and the Independent Philippine Church in the Philippines. Anglicanism here has been true to what is a right ideal for catholicity, the aim that each Christian should belong not to any particular confessional or denominational body, but just to the Catholic Church in the country where he lives.

From the historical point of view, what all the Churches of

the Anglican Communion have in common is that the origin of all of them by one means or another goes back to the Church of England (at least as Anglican Churches); but theologically all that they have in common nowadays is that they are all Catholic Churches independent of the Bishop of Rome. If one studies the reports of the various Lambeth Conferences that have been held ever since the first one in 1867, one can trace a process whereby that which all the Anglican Churches hold in common has gradually been reduced. It began by being the Thirty-Nine Articles and the Book of Common Prayer. The Thirty-Nine Articles soon faded into the background. Most of them are quite irrelevant to Churches in other parts of the world. But gradually the Prayer Book as a bond of union began to disappear also, as the various Anglican Churches began to compile their own liturgies, some of them definitely superior in structure and theology to the Prayer Book of 1662. Ultimately what they all have in common is simply that all are episcopally ordered Churches holding the catholic faith, observing liturgical worship, in communion with each other and independent of the Bishop of Rome. The link of union is the See of Canterbury; they all acknowledge the moral authority of the Archbishop of Canterbury as the head of the Anglican Communion. But the Archbishop of Canterbury is not a Pope; his position is a contingent fact of history. No Anglican in his right senses would regard communion with the See of Canterbury as an essential constituent of catholicity.

An organisation of autonomous national Churches has its dangers. Nationalism can corrupt and pervert true Christianity. The national Church is no more entitled to do anything it chooses than is the nation-state. There is something to be said for having a supranational authority in the Church. To be out of communion with the Bishops of Rome is not an essential of catholicity either. We must consider this further in a later chapter. But we must point out one other implication of Anglicanism's emphasis on national Churches: Anglicans have no right to complain if an Anglican Church is absorbed into a united Church (provided, of course, that the terms of union are otherwise satisfactory). On the contrary, a united Church is much more likely to be representative of the country in which it is situated than is an Anglican Church by itself. One sometimes, for instance, hears Anglican leaders in England lamenting that there are now no Anglicans left in India, because the Church of South India and the Church of North India between them have absorbed them all. If this is the only objection to union, it is quite unjustified. Instead of a small Anglican body we have a much larger, more comprehensive body, retaining the characteristic features of the Catholic Church, and indeed probably improving on the Anglican contribution. Nothing has been lost but the name Anglican. But, when one comes to consider the matter, 'Anglican' should be nothing more than a temporary description of any Church. It should signify those things for which the Church of England has stood ever since the Reformation.

If there is a Church in which what Anglicans stand for is accepted and appreciated, we have no reason to demand that the name 'Anglican' should continue. Indeed the Catholic Church should not need any more descriptive epithets; it should be evangelical certainly, but it does not need the title 'Evangelical'. Nor does it need the title 'Anglican' or 'Roman' or 'Lutheran' or 'Methodist'. It does not even need the title 'Reformed', though it should always be ready to reform itself. We Anglicans ought to be able to contribute to any united Church which we join the ideal of being mere Catholic Christians, not Roman Catholics or Anglo-Catholics or National Catholics. We should set ourselves the task of rescuing that word 'Catholic' from the partisan hands into which it has fallen.

Something like a theology of the Church is thus emerging which would seem to be the right one for Anglicans today. We need not repudiate any important part of our Catholic heritage, but we should abandon once and for all the attempt to un-church any body of Christians. This does not mean a plea for an immediate recognition on the part of the Church of England of all non-episcopal orders. But it does mean that we should be quite ready to accept non-episcopally ordained ministers into our system if the purpose is eventually to establish an episcopally ordered Church in which all will have been ordained by bishops. There seems to be a fear among some Anglicans that even this measure of acceptance of non-episcopal orders would somehow compromise us. The question is, in whose eyes would it compromise us? Not God's, presumably. If we accept that God has used non-episcopal orders as means of grace (including sacramental grace), we can hardly imagine that he would disapprove of our granting them this measure of recognition. It must be a fear of compromising our position *vis-à-vis* the Roman Catholic Church. This fear might have had some justification ten or fifteen years ago, but today Roman Catholic theologians are much less dogmatic about other people's orders than they used to be. There is not much reason to think that a scheme which envisaged the gradual disappearance of non-episcopal orders within a united Church would destroy all hope of future unity with the Roman Catholic Church. It might even strengthen that hope.

That distinguished Anglican theologian of the inter-war years Oliver Quick maintained that, as long as the Church as a whole was divided, all our orders were to that extent (not invalid but) defective.[6] There seems to be much truth in this, as we shall be seeing later on. This line of thought has received confirmation from a continental Roman Catholic theologian, J. Feine. Commenting on the *Decree on Ecumenism* of Vatican II, he writes:

> in the life and teaching of non-catholic communions, aspects of what is Christian have been developed which in Catholicism have been manifested either inadequately or not at all . . . as long as the divisions of the Church endure, it is not possible to bring into being the fullness of catholicity proper to the Church.[7]

He does not apply this to the matter of orders, and perhaps would not be willing to do so; but his words do suggest a fruitful line of thought when it comes to reconciliation between divided communions. We are not compelled to say about the orders of any or every denomination 'they are either totally valid or completely null and void'. We should rather consider what can be made of the ministry of any denomination than busy ourselves with making value-judgements about it. The aim must be to ensure that what God has entrusted of value to each Christian tradition should be made available for the whole Church.

This is not the place to attempt a defence of episcopacy. We do that in our last chapter. But as Anglicans we need not hesitate to commend episcopacy as the only possible basis for a united Church in the realm of order, though we must be prepared for non-Anglicans to interpret episcopacy sometimes in new ways, and indeed to find new values in it. In order that all should share in the riches of all, full intercommunion is certainly needed, and for this there seems to be no other means but one ministry universally recognised. Under these conditions, and in view of the much wider distribution of the catholic elements in the Christian tradition which is a characteristic of the situation today, we are justified in looking on our Anglican conception of the Church as perhaps a focus of Catholic–Protestant unity in the future. There is a tradition of theology and practice which can be appealed to in order to form the basis for such unity. It is what might be called the Reformed Catholic tradition. It can be found underlying the thought of both Luther and Calvin, neither of whom intended to found a new Church *ab ovo*, and both of whom did in practice appeal not to *sola Scripture*, but to the tradition of the Church of the first four centuries. That tradition is the very essence of Anglicanism, and has now appeared in the Church of South India during the quarter century of its existence. It is a tradition which is at the moment making a strong appeal to many thoughtful and well-informed Roman Catholics. It is the only possible tradition upon which any united Church of the future can be founded.

3   Sacraments: baptism

WHY should the Church have sacraments at all? Nothing exactly corresponding to the word 'sacrament' occurs in the New Testament, though the word normally translated 'mystery' comes fairly close to it. It is true that certain rites, notably baptism and the eucharist, are referred to as part of the Church's practice in New Testament times, and the institution of these two rites is attributed to Jesus himself. But we are not unreasonable in asking for something more than the Lord's bare command (if indeed he did command) as a reason for giving such prominence to these two rites. We would like to know how far they are integrally connected with the gospel and the Christian life. Moreover, as we have seen, some Christians actually refrain from observing any sacraments, and one can find a school of thought within Christianity which is very suspicious of any 'sacramental' interpretation of Christianity. One Swiss scholar, the late Martin Werner, even suggested that the observance of the sacraments was the early Church's substitute for the *parousia*, which they had originally expected to take place a few years after Jesus' resurrection.[1] His suggestion has not met with wide acceptance, though there is, as we shall see, a connection between the sacraments and the end time.

The real reason why the Church has always observed the sacraments, and why Christianity is a sacramental religion, is that Christianity is based on the claim that God has redeemed mankind by coming himself in Christ and carrying out that great act of salvation in our midst. Christianity is an incarnational religion; this means that God does not repudiate matter, the visible, the sensible, space–time, but actually uses it as a means of manifesting and communicating himself. D. M.

Baillie well quotes C. S. Lewis in this connection: 'God likes matter; he invented it'.[2] The New Testament writers do not contrast the spiritual with the material. The opposite of 'spiritual' in the New Testament is not 'material', but something else; perhaps 'legal' or 'impersonal' or even 'mechanical'.

This basic truth is well brought out in the Fourth Gospel, a gospel which contains much more considered reflection on the significance of Christ than do the other three. Strangely enough, there is no account of the institution of the eucharist in the Fourth Gospel; but this very fact is probably best explained on the assumption that in John's eyes the whole career of Jesus Christ, from birth to resurrection, was itself a sacrament. It was in fact a revelation and gift of God, using physical things as a medium, to be apprehended by faith. In any case there are passages in the Fourth Gospel which to any unprejudiced reader must be understood as references to baptism and the eucharist: for example 3.5: 'unless one is born of water and the Spirit, he cannot enter the kingdom of God', and 6.53: 'unless you eat the flesh of the Son of man and drink his blood, you have no life in you'. We are led to the same conclusion by a study of the 'signs' in the Fourth Gospel. This is the word which John uses to describe Jesus' miracles; unlike the Synoptic writers John arranges his narrative of the miracles with great care, selecting just those which he thinks suitable to his purpose. It seems likely that he deliberately described seven such 'signs' only, though there is some uncertainty among scholars as to which seven exactly he chose. There is much to be said for the view that in fact he only narrates six 'signs' (this would exclude the walking on the water in 6.16–22, on the ground that he does not present it as a separate 'sign'); the seventh and greatest sign, that which alone could be greater than the raising of Lazarus, is Christ's own cross and resurrection. But this is disputed. The important thing to notice for our purpose is that the 'signs' in John's gospel seem to correspond in the historical life of Jesus to the sacraments in the on-going life of the Church. The 'signs' manifest Christ's glory, meaning his true nature; there is a certain hiddenness about them; and above all they need faith in order to apprehend their true meaning. They are called signs because they do not take place for their own sake but in order to point to something; they point to the true nature of Jesus as the medium of the divine life offered to men. Exactly the same could be said of the sacraments. John's gospel is thus the most sacramental of the four gospels and is itself a strong witness to the importance of sacraments in the life of the Church.

Indeed we can go further than this and say that the Church itself is a sacrament. That is why in this book we have put the sacraments next after the Church and not after the ministry, as is often done. The Church is the means by which the life of Christ is mediated to the world. It is 'an outward and visible sign of an inward and visible grace', to quote the Church Catechism; but we must understand that word 'sign' in a Johannine rather than a modern sense. It is a sign which effects something, not an indication of someone who is absent. The purpose of the Church is to enable mankind to enter into the life, death, and resurrection of Jesus Christ. But the two gospel sacraments do exactly this; they convey and express the life, death, and resurrection of Jesus Christ. Thus Church and sacraments are inseparable. In the case of each sacrament there has been a temptation to divorce it from the life of the Church and turn it into a form of individual insurance or devotion: baptism has too often become a sort of prophylaxis against spiritual (or even physical) dangers, to be received once for all like vaccination and then forgotten. The eucharist has become the individual Christian's act of self-consecration to Christ, best performed quietly and in a select company. Both these temptations are very much present with the Church today (not least the Church of England), but both are corruptions of the sacraments, because both tend to divorce the sacraments from the corporate life of the Church. We may well agree with Karl Rahner when he says that the Church is the primary sacrament.[3]

One sometimes encounters among both Catholics and Protestants a tendency to contrast word and sacraments, to the disparagement of one or the other. Protestant Christianity is alleged to be 'word-Christianity' and Catholic Christianity to be 'sacramental Christianity'. It is true that one effect of the

Reformation, not intended by the Reformers, was that the eucharist ceased to be the centre of Sunday worship for all Protestants, and for many Protestants still today the Lord's Supper is in effect an optional extra observed by those who happen to like that sort of thing. Similarly in the Roman Catholic Church until recently preaching had degenerated into 'the homily'; that is, doctrinal instruction of a classroom nature. But we are witnessing today both a fresh appreciation of the eucharist among Protestants and a renewal of preaching as a declaration of the word of God among Catholics. In fact the two go together, and where one decays the other ultimately suffers also. We cannot do better than quote Karl Rahner once again on this topic: 'the power to preach the word of God by authority of God and of his Christ, and the power to administer the sacraments to men are the two basic powers of the Church which are constiutive of its essence'.[4] He goes on to say that in the sacraments (and he is here thinking of all seven sacraments recognised by the Roman Catholic Church) there is always an efficacious word which accompanies the action.

This leads on to our next question: how many sacraments are there? Traditionally the Church, both Eastern and Western, has distinguished seven sacraments. This has been officially registered as part of Christian doctrine by the Roman Catholic Church; in the East it has never been officially defined but generally accepted. All the Churches of the Reformation, including the Church of England, declined to treat as sacraments any but the two 'gospel' or 'dominical' sacraments, baptism and the eucharist, on the grounds that only these two have been expressly instituted by Christ. D. M. Baillie points out that for a Calvinist a sacrament must have an integral connection with the historical Christ; the action must be accompanied by a divine promise. Only Baptism and the eucharist meet this description.[5] Luther at first inclined to consider penance as a sacrament, but Lutheran practice has unanimously restricted the sacraments to two. Even Catholic custom has always regarded the two gospel sacraments as pre-eminent and constituting a class of their own. In recent times the debate has been somewhat mitigated by a less legalistic approach to the question. We no longer regard Christ as having laid down legislation for the Church. Moreover the doubt as to whether Jesus really did institute baptism (a question which we consider presently) has made modern Christians less anxious to draw a rigid line between the two 'gospel' sacraments and the others.

Nevertheless in this book we intend to restrict ourselves to the consideration of the two great sacraments, ignoring the others. This needs some justification. The other five are: orders, confirmation, penance, unction and marriage. Each must be considered on its merits. Orders may well seem to share the nature of a sacrament, since ordination is a rite wherein Christ acts through the Church to confer grace; it has a sign: the laying on of hands; there is a word to be uttered with the sign. What is lacking is dominical institution. There really is no solid evidence that Christ intended to institute an ordained ministry in the Church. We must consider this more exactly in a later chapter. But orders may well be regarded as a sacramental rite without being formally ranked among the sacraments.

Confirmation lacks many of the features necessary for a sacrament: there is no hint of dominical institution. It is not at all clear at what point in the Church's history confirmation can first be recognised as a distinct element within the rite of initiation, but it certainly cannot be much before the end of the second century. We will come back to this point later. Confirmation has had a chequered history in the Western Church. If it is to be viewed in a sacramental light at all, it must be regarded as an integral part of baptism and not as a sacrament on its own.

Penance is badly named; it should be called absolution, since the penance due as a sign of penitence is not an integral part of absolution. If we define it as the Church's right to grant absolution in Christ's name to penitent sinners, something might be said in defence of its dominical institution. In John 20.23 the risen Christ says to the disciples: 'If you forgive the sins of any, they are forgiven; if you retain the sins of any, they are retained.' Again, in Matt. 16.19, Peter is promised the keys of the kingdom of heaven and Jesus adds 'whatever you bind on earth shall be bound in heaven, and whatever you loose on earth shall be loosed in heaven'. This is repeated to the disciples in Matt. 18.18. Whatever may be said about the historical reliability of these passages, it is quite reasonable to claim that they do witness to the early Church's consciousness of possessing in some sense Christ's authority. But this would point rather towards the Church's power to excommunicate than to the form of private confession which is usually indicated by the word penance. A sacrament, because it is a churchly rite, must have a community reference. It is hard to see how penance as practised today possesses this. There are also difficulties about the sign: there does not seem to be one in this case. So, though we have no reason at all to object to the practice of private confession and absolution (quite the reverse), there does not seem to be any point in calling it a sacrament.

Unction was originally the rite of anointing the sick with oil as a means of mediating divine healing. It has been revived in modern times precisely with this purpose in mind and is proving a blessing throughout the entire Church without any regard to Catholic–Protestant distinctions. But in the mediaeval period this rite changed into a rite for the dying, extreme unction in fact. It has no claim whatever to dominical institution; it can hardly be justified as a sacrament of death.

Finally there is marriage. This, if it is a sacrament, is a very peculiar one, since it is also a natural ordinance. The sacramental element is defended on the basis of a passage in Eph. 5.22–33, where marriage is regarded as a symbol for the relation of Christ to the Church. The suggestion that Christ instituted the sacrament when he attended the marriage at Cana in Galilee is absurd. It seems to me that the Roman Catholic Church has got itself into a formidable theological tangle by insisting that (Catholic) marriage is a sacrament, involving all sorts of unconvincing conclusions about when a marriage is valid and when it is not (for example, the marriage of two pagans performed by a pagan priest is valid; but the marriage of a Roman Catholic and a Protestant performed by a Roman Catholic priest who has not obtained his Church authorities' permission to dispense with the canonical bar is not). There are also difficulties about who performs the

marriage and what is the sign. In short, it seems far more
satisfactory not to try to include marriage among the
sacraments.

We now consider the first of the two gospel sacraments,
baptism. We encounter at once a difficulty. Was baptism
instituted by our Lord? Certainly in Matt. 28.19 the risen Lord
bids the eleven apostles to 'make disciples of all nations,
baptising them in the name of the Father and of the Son and of
the Holy Spirit'. We need not concern ourselves with the fact
that Eusebius' version of this text apparently omitted the
Trinitarian formula and read 'baptising them in my name'.
(Eusebius was a prominent scholar and church historian who
died about 340.) The real problem is: in what sense can we
regard this event as historical? Did the risen Christ command
the eleven to baptise? (It is very unlikely that the Trinitarian
formula goes back to Christ; it witnesses to the belief and
practice of the Church in 'Matthew's' day and area.) We would
be rash to base the dominical origin of baptism on this passage
alone. But there is other evidence to suggest that baptism does
go back to Jesus' own practice.

In the first place we may undoubtedly claim that, as soon as
we have any evidence of the activity of the Church, we find it
practising baptism. This is true of the practice as reflected in
Paul's epistles, and also of the Acts of the Apostles. The
Fourth Gospel claims that both Jesus and his disciples
baptised (see John 3.22; 4.1–2). It is true that in this latter
passage the author of the Fourth Gospel denies that Jesus
himself baptised. But this qualification may be theologically
motivated, or even, as some have suggested (without textual
support), a later comment. In any case there seems no reason
to think that the account of the disciples baptising during
Jesus' life on earth was invented by the author of the Fourth
Gospel. In all probability it is authentic history. If Jesus and
his disciples baptised during his lifetime, we do not need to
look any further for the dominical institution of baptism. It
would be absurd to claim that this baptism had no connection
with John the Baptist's baptism. The one must have been
influenced by the other. But we now know of another non-
conformist movement within the Judaism of the time; the

Qumran Sect. They certainly practised baptism; indeed they required their novices to undergo a series of baptisms. It seems likely then that any renewal movement within Judaism, which would be *ipso facto* dissatisfied with contemporary orthodox Jewish practice, might well require baptism of its adherents as a sign of renewal and allegiance. Consequently the view current fifty years ago which derived Christian baptism from the initiatory rites of the mystery cults is now no longer held by any but a tiny minority. A stronger case could be made for the connection between baptism and the Jewish custom of baptising proselytes from among the Gentiles. But it is not quite certain whether this custom originated before the Christian era. We seem to be able to explain the origin of baptism fairly satisfactorily without supposing a direct link with proselyte baptism.

On the other hand we must not try to dissociate Christian baptism from Jesus' own baptism at the hands of John the Baptist in Jordan, nor from the language he is recorded as using in Mark 10.38 f. The sons of Zebedee make their request for special places in the kingdom and Jesus replies: 'You do not know what you are asking. Are you able to drink the cup that I drink, or to be baptised with the baptism with which I am baptised?' A few verses later he tells them that they will indeed drink his cup and be baptised with his baptism. Baptism here means suffering and death undertaken in accordance with God's will. We remember that we find Paul describing Christian baptism in terms of dying and rising with Christ. And in Eph. 5.25f. Christ is described as having 'loved the Church' and given himself up for her 'that he might sanctify her, having cleansed her by the washing of water with the word'. This rather mysterious passage seems to suggest that Christ in his passion underwent a sort of archetypal baptism on behalf of the Church, which is presumably applied to every new convert afresh as he undergoes baptism accompanied by the baptismal formula. Christ's own baptism in Jordan was sometimes associated in the early Church with the festival of the Epiphany or the New Light: Christ was regarded as having sanctified water as a medium of initiation into the new age. In the light of all this evidence we may be confident that the practice of baptism is deeply rooted in the New Testament, runs right back to the historical ministry of Jesus, and was regarded from the beginning as a means by which the new convert was brought into living contact with the saving action of God in Christ. The parallel with the eucharist cannot fail to strike us.

Baptism figures prominently in Paul's writings; he tells us that in baptism we share in Christ's death and resurrection. No doubt the symbolism of immersion is of significance here: as the convert disappears for a moment beneath the water, so he dies from his old self and rises to new life. It seems likely that according to Paul our baptism is the means by which we appropriate to ourselves Christ's death and resurrection which took place once and for all in history, rather than that we die to the world through Christ in baptism. Certainly for Paul baptism marks the beginning of the Christian life, a decisive event to which the Christian can look back. See 1 Cor. 6.11, where Paul reminds the Corinthian Christians of their degraded condition before conversion and then writes: 'But you were washed, you were sanctified, you were justified in the name of the Lord Jesus Christ and in the Spirit of our God'. Baptism also has an eschatological aspect in Paul; what was begun in baptism will only be completed in the end time. See Rom. 6.5: 'For if we have been united with him in a death like his, we shall certainly be united with him in a resurrection like his'. Some scholars have suggested that Paul did not have a very high regard for baptism, since in 1 Cor. 1.13–17 he protests that Christ did not send him to baptise but to preach the gospel, and points out that he did not baptise many of those who became Christians in Corinth. But a disparaging view of baptism is quite inconsistent with what Paul writes elsewhere, and his reluctance to baptise will be readily understood by anyone with any first-hand acquaintance with areas of the world where Christianity is a new religion making converts frequently. He who first evangelises an area does not necessarily baptise his first converts; a period of teaching and pastoral oversight is always necessary between conversion and baptism. There is also the strange reference to people being 'baptised on behalf of the dead' in 1 Cor. 15.29. This would seem to us to be a misuse of baptism amounting to superstition. It is only a passing reference, however, and Paul does not show any enthusiasm for the custom. There have always been some who have tried to interpret Paul's references to baptism on the assumption that he normally or often means 'baptism of the spirit'; that is, a special gift of the Holy Spirit manifested in prophecy, speaking with tongues, etc., and not water-baptism. But this is not borne out by the evidence. We must beware of reading into Paul's day our modern suspicion of symbolical or ceremonial acts. It is difficult to imagine that any devout Jew of the first century of our era could have thought that an act involving ritual or ceremonial was thereby devoid of moral or spiritual significance. At the same time we must always bear in mind that for Paul, as for all the writers of the New Testament, baptism was always adult baptism; and Paul's rich theology of baptism is orientated towards the baptism of adults, not of children.

There are unmistakable references to baptism in the Fourth Gospel: we have already mentioned 3.5; but many would see a reference to baptism in the episode of the healing of the man born blind in chapter 9, especially as 'illumination' was a figure frequently used for baptism in the early Church. We actually find this usage in Heb. 6.4 and 10.32; in each case we find a warning against relapsing, on the part of those who have been 'enlightened'. There can be no doubt that this means 'baptised'. It is quite unnecessary to underline the frequency of references to baptism in Acts, though perhaps one should issue a warning against any rash attempts to extract a consistent theory of the relation of baptism to the Holy Spirit from the Book of Acts. It does not seem that Luke had any definite theory. In the rest of the New Testament baptism is just as frequently encountered. Many scholars believe that 1 Peter actually includes a baptismal address. Certainly the author's reference to his hearers as 'newborn babes' and his comparison of baptism to Noah's ark (1 Pet. 2.2; 3.20–1) would seem to point in this direction. In Titus 3.5–6 we seem to have the same thought as occurs in Eph. 5.25, that God in Christ's death and resurrection has effected an archetypal baptism for all Christians: 'he saved us, not because of deeds done by us in righteousness, but in virtue of his own mercy, by the washing of regeneration and renewal in the Holy Spirit, which he poured out upon us richly through Jesus Christ our Saviour'. It has also been suggested that if we compare Titus, 1 Peter, and Ephesians we can find the elements of a baptismal liturgical prayer and of ethical instruction which was given to the candidates at baptism. By the end of the New Testament period, therefore, the baptism of new converts has been established as a liturgical rite which was used as an opportunity for doctrinal and moral instruction.

By about the year 200 there is evidence that in certain parts of the Church, notably Rome, the rite of baptism had been supplemented by a number of additional elements, one of which was a laying on of hands on the newly baptised by the bishop (or an anointing with oil) before they received their first communion. Normal practice was that baptism, laying on of hands (or anointing) and first communion all formed one unbroken rite. It was normally performed at only two times in the year, Easter and Pentecost. The ceremony of laying on of hands was not universally observed; there is no trace of it at this period in Syria, and it only seems to have become part of Church practice in Gaul and Spain at a much later time, when Roman customs were superseding local ones. Nor does it seem to have been originally a part of the rite of initiation in the Celtic Church. Similarly in Milan in the late fourth century there does not seem to have been any episcopal laying on of hands though there was a signing of the newly baptised with the sign of the cross by the bishop.

In the East the two parts of the initiation rite were never divided: the only development was that, since it early proved impossible for the bishop to baptise everyone and the rite had to be entrusted to the local presbyter, the task of anointing the newly baptised with oil was also delegated to the local presbyter. This is the custom in the Orthodox Church to this day, though the oil used has been previously blessed by the bishop. Since the vast majority of candidates are infants, this means that the East practises both infant baptism and infant confirmation. Nor do they hesitate to communicate infants. This arrangement certainly means that they have no 'problem of confirmation' as we have in the West. Of course the practice raises other questions which afflict us Westerners, such as whether there is any point in administering sacraments to infants. But, as Dr G. Wainwright well observes, 'the practice of giving total initiation to infants is confined to the Eastern Churches; and these are churches which simply do things, without feeling the need of a neat rationale for them'.[6]

In the West three developments drastically modified the shape of Christian initiation. First, with the Christianisation of the Western world after Constantine, infant baptism came to be the norm and adult baptism the exception. This did not make much difference to the shape of the rite, since the Church in its baptismal order went on for centuries treating helpless infants as if they were responsible adults who happened to be unable to make the responses. But, since infant mortality was very high indeed, and after Augustine the condition of infants dying unbaptised was regarded as dubious and dangerous in the next life, there was strong pressure to have the infant baptised within the first few days after birth. Obviously even in relatively small dioceses the bishop could not be expected to baptise every baby within a few days of birth, so the local presbyter would baptise, and the episcopal laying on of hands would be deferred until the bishop was available. Where it was once deferred, there was an inevitable tendency to wait until the child reached years of discretion (whenever that was). Almost nobody regarded confirmation as essential for salvation or as a ceremony without which baptism was dangerously incomplete. Secondly, it became increasingly rare to confine baptism to the two seasons of Easter and Pentecost. As long as most people were baptised at these seasons, episcopal laying on of hands (and indeed episcopal baptism) could still be the rule, since the candidates could wait until Easter or Pentecost, and then attend the diocesan church, or some other major church in the diocese where there was a baptistery. But once baptism was divorced from the two great seasons the episcopal part of the rite could not possibly accompany it. In some areas (Anglo-Saxon England for example) we actually find legislation attempting to enforce the baptism of infants within a few days of birth.

Thirdly, outside Italy dioceses as they were formed tended to coincide with tribal areas, and bishops ultimately became integrated into the feudal system as barons. This had the effect of further removing the bishop from the local church. He became a remote official who could only be expected to visit any given area at the rarest of intervals, if at all. As a baron or high civil servant he was constantly in request for transacting the business of the state; his pastoral functions suffered. Western Europe finally settled down into a state of affairs in which every infant was baptised as soon as possible after birth. Confirmation was only administered from about the seventh year onward, and even then depended for most children on whether the bishop (or a bishop) was likely to be in the vicinity. It is plain that bishops would often confirm by the roadside, from horseback, or in a field; often blessing the children from afar rather than laying hands on each individual. There can be no doubt that a very great number of people were never confirmed at all. In as far as the faithful did receive communion (a sufficiently rare event for most), it was not normally made dependent on confirmation having been administered first. Efforts were made from time to time to regularise this situation. Archbishop Peckham of Canterbury in 1281 tried to enforce confirmation by ruling that no one should be admitted to communion who had not previously been confirmed; but even he had to modify the rule so much (for those in danger of death; for those who have been prevented from receiving confirmation by some reasonable cause), that it soon became a dead letter.

The separation from baptism of the laying on of hands meant that a new theological significance had to be thought out for the second rite. This the mediaeval theologians found in the concept of confirmation: the laying on of hands by the bishop imparted strength for living the Christian life. Thomas Aquinas calls it the sacrament of growth; others suggested that it conferred grace to witness to Christ. Whatever the historical antecedents of the rite, it was obviously a useful custom in practice, since it would be employed in conjunction with instruction in the faith at a period of a child's life when he is about to meet the test of puberty and adolescence.

Thus the Western Church generally, and the Church of England in particular, finds itself today with an originally unified rite of initiation that has been split into two parts. The practice of the Western Church with regard to confirmation has not been uniform or self-consistent, and it is vain to expect to be able to devise a theology which will make sense of confirmation at every period and in every area in the West. It is true that there is a school of Anglican theologians, supported to some extent by some Roman Catholics, who maintain that the laying on of hands (to which anointing with oil may be regarded as an alternative) always was an integral part of the rite of Christian initiation, and that therefore those who have not been confirmed have not really been initiated into the Christian Church. They meet the historical objection that there is no evidence for the laying on of hands etc. before 200 by arguing that: (a) there are indications before 200 that can be construed as evidence; and (b) the evidence for the universal use of water-baptism before 200 is also ambiguous. But their historical arguments under either (a) or (b) are not very impressive and have convinced few. And the theological implications of this view strictly applied are appalling: only a small minority of those whom through the ages and right up to the present day we have been accustomed to regard as Christians can really be accounted as such. All the others (who did not receive episcopal confirmation by the actual laying on of hands) seem to have got stuck in the very doorway of the household of faith.

Before we attempt briefly to present a theology of baptism suitable for our present age, we should honestly face the two great difficulties. We can express them in the form of two questions: What should we do about confirmation? and what should we do about the baptism of infants?

Serious objections can be raised against the baptism of infants. Ever since the Reformation there has been a substantial body of Christians who refused to practise paedo-baptism, deferring baptism until an age of discretion, and usually then requiring baptism by immersion. Most of these Christians are to be found in the various Baptist Churches, but some non-Baptist denominations also reject paedo-baptism. In the first place, how can an infant receive baptism as it is understood in the New Testament? Baptism is supposed to be the moment when the individual enters the Church of his own free will, has his sins forgiven and receives the grace of God to begin the Christian life. How can any of these things be said of a helpless infant? Again, opponents of paedo-baptism would claim that there is no clear evidence of infant baptism taking place in the Church before AD 200, and that then we find Tertullian protesting against it. Thirdly they would stress the danger of a purely magical view of baptism resulting from the baptism of infants, and they could indeed produce much evidence from history and contemporary practice to support this. Finally, as far as concerns the present practice of the Church of England, it could be said with a great deal of truth that our habit of baptising almost indiscriminately all babies presented for baptism merely degrades the sacrament. Whatever can be said in defence of paedo-baptism, it could well be argued that our present policy of baptising infants, the majority of whom by all human calculation will not be brought up in anything like a Christian environment, is indefensible.

To this it can be replied that baptism has always been accepted as the method of becoming a Christian and entering the Church. Are there no such persons as Christian children? Christ is recorded as having blessed children in arms; presumably therefore they are capable of receiving some spiritual benefits. One hesitates to make very much use of arguments from the psychology of the unconscious, but it is nevertheless clear from the researches of psychologists that even the smallest infant is very far from being a purely passive recipient: response of a more than automatic kind takes place from the moment of birth. Though there is no doubt that the practice of infant baptism has been abused, there are circumstances in which it is meaningful and can be looked back on in later life as a significant event. The anniversary of the baptism can be observed (better still the baptism can be arranged to take place on some rather more significant day in the year; I had the good fortune to be baptised on the Feast of the Epiphany; this was mere luck, as it meant nothing to my parents; but one of my children was also baptised at Epiphany, deliberately this time); a Christian milieu must be there to welcome the child; confirmation may be looked forward to as the time when baptism is particularly remembered and accepted—in these circumstances infant baptism is by no means an empty rite. But note the conditions! As far as concerns evidence for infant baptism in the early Church, it is impossible to say with any certainty whether, when whole households are described as being baptised, this includes small children. On the whole it seems likely it did. But early Christian practice varied: in some circles it seems that children born to Christian parents in the early Church were never baptised even in adulthood. They were regarded as holy by birth (compare 1 Cor. 7.14: 'the unbelieving husband is consecrated through his wife, and the unbelieving wife is consecrated through her husband. Otherwise, your children would be unclean, but as it is they are holy'). What is entirely lacking is any evidence from the early Church for present Baptist practice, delaying the baptism of children till they reached years of discretion. There were indeed many people in the third and fourth centuries AD who delayed their baptism deliberately. But this was from quite different motives: they believed that baptism conferred a complete forgiveness of sins, and they calculated that if they postponed their baptism till they were on their death-bed they could enter the next world with a clean sheet. Finally, defenders of paedo-baptism would commend it because it appropriately emphasises that in baptism the initiative is with God not man.

Thus the baptism of infants can reasonably be defended in our present circumstances; but not, I believe, the way in which we practise it in the Church of England. I believe that we must plead guilty to the Baptists' accusation that by baptising multitudes of infants who have no reasonable prospect of being brought up in a Christian environment we are degrading the sacrament. It is true that our present practice has its defenders, who plead eloquently and sincerely for the right of every baby to be baptised as long as the Church of England continues to be the Church of the English people.[7] I can only record my impression after reading such defences that their authors are living in an age that is rapidly passing away, and that the

Church of England must accept the position of a minority group. One advantage of this development, however regrettable it be in other ways, is that we should now be able to give baptism its true place in the economy of the Church, and that means a radical alteration in our present practice.

We may then describe baptism as the beginning of the Christian life: the person baptised is first brought into association with the death and resurrection of Christ and begins to drink his cup and be baptised with his baptism; that is, to live the Christian life. This is how the life begins; but it must, if it is to continue, be sustained by all the means of grace, prayer, Bible-reading, self-discipline, and supremely communicating at the eucharist, where the Christian life is nourished, expressed, and actualised. The objection to the indiscriminate baptism of infants is not that at such a baptism 'nothing happens', but that a beginning is made which is never continued. It is a little reminiscent of normal Sunday worship in the Swedish Lutheran Church: the priest enters clad in what are plainly eucharistic vestments. He conducts what is in origin the preliminaries of the eucharistic liturgy; he advances to the altar. But at this point the service comes to an unexpected conclusion: what looked like becoming a eucharist has ended before fulfilment.

It follows that we ought in the Church of England to control more carefully our present practice of baptising all babies who are presented for baptism. How this control is to be exercised it is not the function of this book to suggest. It is not an easy problem; the parish priest should not be left with the invidious task of deciding what is and what is not likely to constitute a Christian environment. The problem therefore must be tackled at diocesan level.

We should face honestly the fact that the Western Church has behaved quite inconsistently about its practice of confirmation. The primitive initiation rite has been split into two parts; they cannot be joined again except in the case of adult baptisms, when indeed they ought to be reunited. In such instances permission should be given to the local presbyter to lay on hands in confirmation if (but only if) the bishop is not available. There is nothing unprecedented about a presbyter administering confirmation: very frequent examples can be found in the mediaeval Church, and the Roman Catholic Church still admits the practice occasionally today. In our country the number of people who have not been baptised in infancy and who come to faith in adult life is certainly increasing. The parish priest should welcome this, not deplore it. It gives him an opportunity of manifesting something like the primitive order of initiation: adult candidates should be baptised, confirmed, and receive their first communion all in one service, which will be (one hopes) a main Sunday service. It is a fine opportunity for showing forth the true pattern of Christian initiation.

We should not totally rule out the possibility of infant confirmation: it may be defensible where there is a strongly Christian family and a firmly Christian environment. But it would be disastrous if we were to solve our 'problem of confirmation' by making confirmation a usual adjunct of infant baptism. We do not want nominal confirmation added to nominal baptism. There are already too many people in England whose confirmation was nominal enough in all conscience; we do not want to add to their number.

As long as we continue to baptise infants (and there is no human likelihood of very many clergy in the Church of England discontinuing the practice), we must have the rite of confirmation. This is not because the rite is an essential part of Christian initiation, but because infant baptism requires that there be a point in the life of the adult, or the nearly adult, when he can accept for himself the responsibilities of the Christian life. This is witnessed to by the fact that nearly all the Churches of the Reformation which discarded confirmation as a sacrament have nevertheless been compelled to introduce a ceremony of 'full church membership' or some such thing. But we should feel free to arrange this rite of confirmation at the moment when it is likely to be most needed and most effective; and the tendency today is to put it later rather than earlier. It might well form the climax of a course of instruction in the Christian life, perhaps coming at 16 or 17 rather than as at present at 12 or 14. This does not mean a devaluation of confirmation: it is still a rite of growth. It is still a means of grace. It can still be an opportunity for the near-adult Christian to meet the diocesan bishop. Confirmation will never disappear from the life of the Church because it is obviously needed. The experience of the Church of South India bears this out: at union in 1947 confirmation (whether by the bishop or by the local presbyter) was to be a voluntary rite. But in the course of that Church's history it has certainly been widely adopted by those elements in the Church who did not previously use it.

We must however no longer insist on confirmation as the essential preliminary to first communion. As we have seen, this has never been the invariable practice of the Western Church despite efforts to enforce it. In the Roman Catholic Church today first communion is not tied to confirmation, and often precedes it by some years. We will probably find ourselves making a distinction between the families of regular church-goers on the one hand, and those (whether children or adults) who have come into the life of the Church on their own or in non-family groups. The child of the family who are regular communicants should be allowed to receive Communion as soon as his family and the parish priest believe it is appropriate (obviously there will have to be some instruction beforehand). Confirmation can then await near-adulthood. In the case of others, it may be best to insist on confirmation before first communion. But it would be foolish to lay down rigid regulations. It is very much to be hoped that Christians from other denominations who have been baptised and are regular communicants in their own denomination, if they wish to join the Church of England, will not be required to undergo confirmation. Such a demand directly implies that confirmation is a *sine qua non* for true, correct, or full membership of the Church, a position which, as we have seen, is historically and theologically indefensible.

Baptism in fact as one of the two great sacraments of the Church is urgently in need of rehabilitation in the West today. The increasing secularisation of daily life, the dropping off of the last official ties between Church and state, should actually assist this process. No doubt in a situation of Christendom baptism as a sacrament is bound to suffer. In order to see what baptism can mean one has to travel to countries which have never been part of Christendom. I once had the experience of assisting at the baptism of ninety persons at once; the outcaste community in a village in Andhra Pradesh in South India had decided to become Christian and had received six months of preparation with a resident teacher. It was a most moving and significant ceremony: they came up to the font (a huge basin of water) by families, from aged grandmothers to tiny children. They also all received new names, Christian ones, free from association with Hindu deities. One did most certainly have the sense of a new life beginning. We cannot expect all our baptisms in England to be like that, but we can strive to make baptism much more meaningful than it has been for many centuries among us. We can also heed the words of George Every when he urges us to 'think of baptism and the eucharist as two parts of one complex action, essentially interdependent in the end as in the beginning . . . baptism without the eucharist is incomplete, an unfinished rite'.[8] In baptism, as in the eucharist, we proclaim the death and resurrection of the Lord. Both sacraments are intended to enable us in some sense to reproduce that death and that life in our lives. The one is an all-important beginning; a new departure. The other is the means whereby his death and resurrection are constantly renewed in us.

4 Sacraments: the eucharist

PERHAPS no question in New Testament studies is more obscure and confused than is that which concerns the origin of the eucharist. The difficulty is not so much that there is a lack of evidence, as that the evidence seems to be conflicting and puzzling. At the very outset we encounter a manifest contradiction between the Synoptic Gospels and the Fourth Gospel about the actual day on which the Last Supper took place. We must bear in mind that for religious purposes the Jews reckoned the day as beginning at sunset. The Synoptic writers evidently believed that the twenty-four hours which covered the Last Supper, the arrest in Gethsemane, the trial of Jesus, his crucifixion, death and burial, coincided with the Passover festival day. John on the other hand goes out of his way to emphasise that all these events took place on the Day of Preparation, the day before the Passover Day proper. Again, although the Synoptists and Paul witness to the institution at the Last Supper of a rite commemorating Jesus' atoning death, there are indication in Acts and in the very early document known as the *Didache* that early Christians observed a fellowship meal which seemed to have no reference to Jesus' death, but to be rather an anticipation of the messianic banquet. Scholars, in their attempts to unravel this complicated problem, have drawn on the resources of astronomy, rabbinic lore, Hellenistic religion, and the earliest liturgies of the Church. We cannot possibly hope to decide all the issues in a work such as this one. We must content ourselves with stating certain conclusions which, we believe, would gain the assent of a respectable number of scholars.

First, the Last Supper was not a bolt from the blue. During the Lord's ministry he must have held fellowship meals with his disciples, of which we find traces in the various accounts in the gospels of the feeding of multitudes with bread. In all four gospels these narratives have undoubted eucharistic overtones (not least in the Fourth Gospel). This does strongly suggest what we might call an ancestry for the eucharist in these meals. We cannot determine with any certainty the nature of these meals (not *Haburah* meals, it seems, which were fellowship meals presided over by a teacher, with his disciples); but we can be reasonably sure that the eucharist originated in the historical ministry of Jesus himself, not solely on the last night of his life on earth.

Secondly, we cannot ignore the work of J. Jeremias, the great German expert on the Aramaic background to the gospels. In his important book *The Eucharistic Words of Jesus*[1] he insists that the Last Supper was a Passover meal held on the Passover Day. We should look at his reconstruction of the way in which, he believes, Jesus gave a new interpretation to the Passover ritual. He sets it out as follows:

A. *The preliminary course*
   a blessing over the cup
   the bitter herbs etc. were eaten

B. *The Passover Liturgy*
   the account of the Passover story by the head of the family
   the first part of the Passover Hymn (Psalms 113–114)
   the second cup is passed round

C. *The Main Meal*
   grace is said over the unleaven bread
   *here Jesus said 'This is my body'
   the meal is eaten
   a prayer is said over the third cup
   *here Jesus said: 'This is my blood'

D. *The Conclusion*
   the second part of the Passover Hymn (Psalms 115–118)
   (compare Mark 14.26 'when they had sung a hymn')
   praise over the fourth cup.

We should notice that, if this is the correct order, the so-called 'words of institution' were uttered as Jesus gave the bread and wine to his disciples. They are therefore not, strictly speaking, words of consecration but of administration.

Thirdly, however, we must not ignore the fact that an earlier German scholar, Hans Lietzmann, had put forward a somewhat different account of the origin of the eucharist.[2] According to him, the eucharist was originally a simple fellowship meal, 'the breaking of the bread', held by the disciples after the resurrection in memory of their Lord and in continuation of the meals which they had enjoyed during the days of his flesh. It was Paul who, as a result of a special revelation (1 Cor. 11.23: 'For I received from the Lord what I also delivered to you, that the Lord Jesus Christ on the night that he was betrayed took bread . . . etc.'), turned the simple fellowship meal into a memorial of the Last Supper and thereby connected it with Christ's atoning death. Lietzmann suggested that Paul was partly at least inspired to do this by his observation of the religious meals which were a feature of the pagan Mystery Cults of his day. This last suggestion has not been adopted by modern scholars: it is most unlikely that either the Mystery Cults or the religious meals of the Qumran Sect had any direct influence on the origin of the eucharist. As A. R. C. Leaney writes: 'scholars surely ought to give up the fantasy that the scrolls explain the Eucharist. . . . Nothing whatever is said [in the Qumran documents] even faintly resembling the words of institution reported as used by Jesus at the Last Supper.'[3] But Lietzmann can certainly bring significant evidence to suggest that in the early Church the ritual meal was not necessarily connected with Christ's atoning death: the practice of 'the breaking of the bread' in Acts; the absence of any mention of the memorial of Christ's death in the shorter text of Luke 22.19f (the shorter text stops at 'This is my body' and omits the whole of verse 20); the (apparently) eucharistic prayers in the *Didache*, which do not refer to the Lord's death—all these suggest that there was an alternative tradition about the eucharist to that provided by Paul and Mark.

Perhaps we would be justified in drawing three solid conclusions from the confusing evidence:[4]

1. The Last Supper was a Passover meal, whatever the day on which it was observed. It was the last of the fellowship meals at which the Lord was present in the flesh, and the Lord gave it a new interpretation for the new age which his death was to inaugurate.

2. It took some time for the tradition based on the Last Supper to integrate with the 'fellowship meals' tradition. One of the difficulties about the assumption that the Last Supper was a new Passover is that we would expect it to be celebrated like the old Passover, only once a year; but already in Paul's practice it is a weekly rite. Perhaps the influence of the 'fellowship meals' made for this result.

3. The rite has existed in the Church from the very earliest days and undoubtedly goes back to the practice of Jesus himself.

In so far as we find a theology of the eucharist anywhere in the New Testament, it is in Paul's writings that we must look for it. In 1 Cor. 10.1–13 Paul draws a parallel between the experiences of Israel in the wilderness and the life of the Church of his day. Here the manna and the water from the rock correspond to the eucharist: we learn that Christ was the source of both the manna and the water from the rock and was present by their means. The analogy would also suggest that the existence of the sacrament does not destroy the reality of the 'elements' by which grace is mediated: the manna and the water really sustained the Israelites physically as well as being spiritual nourishment. In 1 Cor. 11.27–32 Paul, having repeated the tradition about the eucharist which he received when he became a Christian, makes some significant comments on it. In particular he warns against unworthy reception: 'Whoever, therefore, eats the bread or drinks the cup of the Lord in an unworthy manner will be guilty of profaning the body and blood of the Lord. . . . For anyone who eats and drinks without discerning the body eats and drinks judgement upon himself.' Some scholars have suggested that this means: 'He who fails to recognise the Lord's body in the elements finds that they turn to deadly poison.' But, apart from the fact that common experience shows that this is not the case, such a view is incompatible with the passage we have referred to in 1 Cor. 10.1–13: there some of the Israelites ate and drank unworthily, but they were not poisoned. It makes better sense to take 'discerning the body' as we have done in Chapter 1: he who partakes unworthily fails to recognise the Church signified in the rite, and thereby sins against the Lord, whose body the Church is. One could draw further theological conclusions about the eucharist from occasional references in the rest of the New Testament; for example in Heb. 6.4. we find a phrase 'those who have tasted the heavenly gift'. This surely means the eucharist; it reminds us that in the early Church the eucharist was 'the antepast of heaven'. The Jacobite Christians of Malabar, whose tradition goes back probably to the third century AD, call the eucharist 'the Holy Qurbana', the same word as 'Korban' in Mark 7.11; that is, gift.

Whatever else the eucharist is, it is a memorial. But we must understand this word in a Jewish rather than a modern sense: when the Jew made a memorial of what God had done for his people in the past, he entered into the experience of the past and in some sense relived it or made it contemporary. He did not merely look back on a past event or events as we do in a 'Memorial Service'. One rabbinic text says of the narrative of the exodus which formed an essential part of the Passover service: 'Everyone must regard himself as if he had come out from Egypt.' So when Christians celebrate the memorial of Christ's death and resurrection, they do not merely remember a past event: they enter into those past events and make them their own in contemporary time.

There does not seem to have been any one agreed name for the rite in very early times. The name 'Lord's Supper' comes from 1 Cor. 11.20: 'When you meet together, it is not the Lord's supper that you eat.' But Paul means that owing to the misbehaviour of the Corinthians the supper they eat cannot possibly be described as belonging to the Lord. He is not apparently referring to it by its accustomed name. The name 'eucharist', which we use throughout this work, first occurs in the *Didache* and in Ignatius of Antioch (martyred *c.* AD 110); it is a most appropriate one, because as soon as we have any evidence of the way in which the rite was celebrated, we find that the central part of the rite, as far as concerns what is said, consists in a long prayer of thanksgiving in which God is thanked not only for the death of Christ, but for all his saving acts towards men, creation, redemption, sanctification. You will have noted the big place which blessings or graces play in the Passover ritual. The Jewish way of saying grace was to thank God. Thus an ancient Jewish grace runs: 'Blessed be Thou, O Lord, King of the ages, who bringest forth food from the earth.' The blessings in the Christian Passover that was the eucharist early took the form of thanking God for his saving acts in Christ. This would also fit in with the Passover *Haggada*, or narrative of the exodus. Christians in the eucharist remembered with thanksgiving the new and greater deliverance which God in Christ brought about for all men. Thus, when we encounter the very first description of the eucharist in Justin about AD 150 in Rome, we find that it consists of the following sequence:

1. A reading of Scripture
2. A sermon from the president (probably the bishop)
3. Intercessions
4. Offering of the bread and wine
5. The Thanksgiving Prayer ended by the people's Amen
6. Communion.

Notice that by now the meal element has completely dropped out. Justin does not lay much emphasis on the rôle of the president of the eucharist. Indeed he has a very fine grasp of the priesthood of the whole Church, for he writes elsewhere:[5] 'We Christians are the true high-priestly race of God, as God himself witnesses when he says that in every place we shall offer amongst the Gentiles sacrifices well pleasing to him and pure' (Justin is referring to Mal. 1.11, which he regards as a prophecy of the eucharist).

Fifty years later we have an actual text of the eucharistic prayer from Hippolytus' *Apostolic Tradition*; it represents the local tradition of Rome, or at any rate what Hippolytus thought the local tradition of Rome ought to be. The prayer is too long to quote, but we reproduce Gregory Dix's summary of it:[6]

(a) Address: Relation of the Father to the Eternal Word
(b) Thanksgiving for Creation through the Word
(c) Thanksgiving for the Incarnation of the Word
(d) Thanksgiving for Redemption through the Passion of the Word
(e) Statement of Christ's purpose in instituting the eucharist
(f) Statement of his institution of the eucharist
(g) Statement of his command to repeat the action
(h) Offering of the elements
(i) Prayer for the effects of communion
(j) Doxology.

We observe that the thanksgiving is for the whole divine action, not only for the death, still less merely for the institution of the eucharist. The 'words of institution' are incorporated into the thanksgiving, and do not seem to be regarded as the essential core of the prayer. Indeed in some eastern liturgies of the third century AD we have a thanksgiving prayer which does not actually contain 'the words of institution'. There is in Hippolytus' liturgy an offering of the elements, but it seems to be closely connected with the thanksgiving. There is no suggestion that we offer Christ.

The actual text of the old Canon of the Mass in Latin (until recently the form which the great majority of Roman Catholics followed), is not so different from Hippolytus' order as to be unrecognisable as its descendant. Admittedly the inter-cessions have now been inserted into the thanksgiving part, and the focus of the rite seems to be more concentrated on the thought of Christ's death as an expiation for sin than on the joyful thanksgiving for deliverance which is the keynote of the early service. But a much more radical change began to affect the way the rite was used and the theology attached to it. The change may be said to have begun as early as Cyprian (martyred AD 258); he was anxious to link the ministry of the new dispensation with that of the old, and he observed of course that the Old Testament priesthood was chiefly engaged in offering sacrifices. He therefore suggested that the sacrifice which the Christian priest offers in the eucharist is the death of Christ. This was elaborated in subsequent centuries, so that by about the year 1500 in the West it was popularly held that the priest offers the sacrifice of Christ in the mass on behalf of the living and the dead. With the spread of the Church westward and northward the service was never translated out of Latin into the new vernaculars that were growing up, so that well before the year 1000 the language of the rite had become incomprehensible to all who were not educated, and almost no one but a cleric was educated.

A still more drastic change from the primitive service appeared when, after Constantine's recognition of the Church in 311, the custom of the faithful receiving communion at the Sunday eucharist began to be abandoned. Despite the protests of Church leaders, the laity gradually slipped into the position of non-communicating bystanders, except on certain great occasions in the year. In the meantime the celebrant had begun to absorb all the important rôles in the service, and the part of the people dropped out of use. The mass came to be regarded as something which the priest did on behalf of a passive laity. This tendency was accentuated by the custom of daily masses, and of offering masses on behalf of the dead. A rich man would leave a legacy to ensure that a priest celebrated a mass on his behalf every day. Finally we should note that even on those rare occasions when the laity did take communion they were not normally given the cup at all. For reasons both of hygiene and of reverence, communion in one kind from about the twelfth century onward became the usual custom for the laity. By the fifteenth century it was regarded as illegitimate that the laity should receive the cup. Thus, if we review the development of the eucharist in the West from about the year 300 to about the year 1500, we find that what had been a joyful celebration on the part of the people of God of God's deliverance had turned into a mysterious rite conducted by a priest in an ancient language for the purpose of enabling individual Christians to be rid of their sins.

Naturally during these centuries theologians had speculated about the mode by which Christ was present to his people in the eucharist. In the earlier centuries under the influence of the Platonic tradition the tendency had been to interpret the sacrament in terms of symbolism: the consecrated elements were effective symbols of spiritual realities. But with the rise of Aristotelianism in the thirteenth century a more realistic philosophy prevailed, and this finally produced the doctrine of transubstantiation, first defined in 1215, but elaborated later by Thomas Aquinas. According to this doctrine, when the 'words of consecration' ('this is my body ... this is my blood') are pronounced by the priest the substance of the bread and wine is changed into the substance of the body and blood of Christ, though the accidents (external appearance, etc.) remain unchanged. The doctrine was as much an attempt to avoid a crude literalism about the elements as to emphasise the objective presence of Christ in the elements. But it only makes sense if one accepts the Thomistic categories of substance and accident.

In the East a parallel but not identical development took place. It is true that the Eastern Church did translate the liturgy into the vernacular in the days of its evangelisation of eastern Europe and Russia: but it has remained in that vernacular (Old Slavonic) ever since, and today this language and the Hellenistic Greek in which worship is conducted in Greek-speaking lands are equally incomprehensible to the laity. The abandonment of frequent communion also affected the Eastern Church. The doctrine of transubstantiation has never been officially accepted, but something very like it would be acknowledged by most Orthodox theologians. Moreover, as a parallel to the 'secret' utterance of the canon of the mass by the priest in the pre-Vatican II Roman Catholic Church, most Orthodox Churches today have an *iconostasis*. This is a wall built across the church to separate sanctuary from nave. The essential parts of the rite take place behind the wall out of sight of the congregation. But the wall is pierced by three doors, and the celebrants come out through these doors at various crucial points in the service, most notably after the consecration, when the consecrated elements are exhibited for the adoration of the people.

On the other hand there are certain marked differences from the Western development: the people's part has not disappeared. By singing, by responses, by prayers the people follow the action of the liturgy. Indeed the Orthodox Church probably affords the most corporate and participant worship to its adherents in all Christendom: the icons of the saints, most especially of the Blessed Virgin Mary, mediate a sense of community and family worship. There is far more scope for thanksgiving in the liturgy and the note of joy and praise is much more obvious than in the old Latin mass. Communion, on the rare occasions when the laity receive it, is in both kinds. There are no private masses for the dead, daily mass is rare, and adoration of the reserved sacrament outside the liturgy is unknown. Moreover Orthodox theologians have a different theology of consecration: for them the moment of consecration is at the *epiclesis*, or invocation of the Holy Spirit upon the elements. As a liturgical feature this is not found earlier than the fourth century, but it has genuine theological significance, as we shall be seeing.

The Reformers reacted violently against the mass: in theology the two great targets of their criticism were the sacrifice of the mass and the doctrine of transubstantiation. In the realm of practice, they were determined to make the language of worship comprehensible to the people, to restore the people's part in the liturgy, and to bring back communion in both kinds. Luther, Calvin, and Cranmer all desired to restore weekly communion if they could, or at least more frequent communion. They all objected to non-communicating attendance.

The actual doctrines which the various Reformers offered in place of the sacrifice of the mass and transubstantiation need not concern us. As George Every well remarks, they attributed to Christ exactly the sort of sacrifice which late mediaeval thought attributed to the priest; something made by him to God for the people but without the people.[7] They did succeed in translating the liturgy into the various vernaculars; they did to some extent succeed in bringing the people into the action of the liturgy. But they had only a very vague idea of what early Church worship had actually been like, and they therefore tended to concentrate the centre of the eucharistic rite on the actual words of consecration, thereby perpetuating a mediaeval misconception. In effect they either drastically reduced, or removed altogether, the element of thanksgiving.

Because of their horror of the sacrifice of the mass, the element of offering was played down. The characteristic Reformation emphasis on man's sinfulness did not fail to make itself felt. As far as concerns the Church of England, this meant that, even after the modification of Cranmer's rite of 1552 effected in 1662, we had a eucharistic liturgy in which the thanksgiving prayer (which began at the *Sursum Corda*) was abruptly broken off and the Prayer of Humble Access, reminding us of our sinful condition, inserted. When the main theme of the rite is resumed with the so-called Prayer of Consecration, the note of thanksgiving has faded out, attention is concentrated on Christ's death as the means of our redemption (with no memorial whatever of his resurrection), and the 'words of institution' are isolated and utilised as a consecratory formula in a style which can only be called late-mediaeval. The early belief that it is the thanksgiving which consecrates is totally incompatible with the Prayer Book eucharist.

The Reformers did not succeed in restoring frequent communion. What has happened was that, when it became clear that the people were not willing to communicate every Sunday, rather than revert to non-communicating attendance, the authorities in the Reformed Churches decided that the eucharist would only be celebrated on those few occasions in the year when the people were willing to communicate in large numbers. So in all the Reformed Churches a substitute for normal Sunday mass had to be found. In Lutheran countries it was the 'dry mass', in Reformed countries the preaching service, and in England Morning and Evening Prayer.

It must therefore be admitted that in their attempt to restore the primitive eucharist all the Reformers failed disastrously. They removed many abuses, but the reformed rites were mere shadows of the early eucharist, often shrunk to an almost superstitious concentration on the words of institution. The eucharist was no longer the central act of the Church's worship. In too many areas of Protestantism it became nothing more than a pious exercise indulged in by the devout few.

However the end of the nineteenth century saw a promise of better things: there began in the Roman Catholic Church what was called the 'liturgical movement'. This was a movement, fostered by the Benedictines and encouraged by Pope Pius X (reigned 1903–14), to restore active participation by the people in the official worship of the Church. Parallel to this there developed historical research into the nature and shape of the early eucharist, a development which, unlike contemporary research on the New Testament itself, showed a remarkable consensus among scholars of all traditions. It thus became gradually clear that, as far as resemblance to the eucharistic pattern of the Church of the first four centuries was concerned, all the main traditions of the modern Church were about equally distant from the primitive pattern. The liturgical movement has now spread to all parts of the Church. It could be said that Anglicanism was better prepared for it than were the other Churches of the Reformation because the Oxford Movement, developing into the Anglo-Catholic movement as the nineteenth century progressed, focused attention on the eucharist as the proper centre of the Church's Sunday worship. This shift of interest did not at first make for liturgical renewal: on the contrary, it imposed upon many Anglicans a novel pattern of Sunday worship whereby the devout made their communion early in the morning at a said eucharist with a relatively small attendance (reminiscent of the 'low mass' of contemporary Roman Catholicism), then at the main service the larger number of the faithful were encouraged to attend a sung celebration with more or less ceremonial at which none but the celebrants were expected to communicate. This is a much less common pattern in the Church of England today, but it has left a legacy in the shape of the 'eight o'clock communion'. When this service follows the Prayer Book rite it is just about as unlike a normal eucharist of the early Church as any service could be without ceasing to be a eucharist altogether. However, we will examine the proper shape and pattern of the eucharist in greater detail presently, contenting ourselves for the moment with pointing out that the liturgical movement has now turned into a great eucharistic revival throughout the entire Church. Protestants of all traditions are now experiencing this revival and are producing orders of communion which bear a most marked resemblance to each other and to those produced by the Catholic side of

Christendom. The only major part of the Church as yet apparently wholly uninfluenced by this movement is the Orthodox Church.

It will be remembered that the two great targets of the Reformers' criticism were 'the sacrifice of the mass' and the doctrine of transubstantiation. All the drastic alterations which they made in the celebration of the eucharist were intended to reform what they regarded as these two abuses. It can be said without exaggeration that today, thanks to careful and balanced theological study and discussion by Catholic, Anglican, and Protestant theologians, these two great bugbears of the Reformers need no longer be the cause of serious division between Catholics and Protestants. As far as the doctrine of the sacrifice of the mass is concerned, for the past fifty years or so Roman Catholic theologians have been attempting to understand the concept of sacrifice in such a way as not to confine it exclusively to the destruction of the victim. They have also been trying to define the eucharistic sacrifice in sacramental and spiritual, rather than in historical and material terms. The consequence is that most modern theologians of the Roman Catholic Church would emphasise as much as any Protestant that Christ's sacrifice upon the cross cannot be repeated. George Every's statement would probably be accepted by most modern Roman Catholic theologians when he defines the eucharist 'not as a repetition or reiteration of the sacrifice of Christ, but as the sacramental means whereby his death and resurrection, and our baptism, are renewed in us'.[8] See also the Agreed Statement on the Eucharist' recently issued by theologians of the Roman Catholic Church and of the Anglican Communion, which expresses the relationship thus: 'The Eucharist is given us as a means by which the atoning sacrifice of Christ is made effective in the Church.'[9] In just the same vein an agreed statement between Roman Catholic and Lutheran theologians coming from the USA in 1967 says specifically that Christ's sacrifice on the cross cannot be repeated.[10] Consequently it is perfectly reasonable to claim that the question of the sacrifice of the mass, though there is room for very varying emphasis, need not be a matter of serious division among Christians in the West. One of the two great divisive issues concerning the eucharist need no longer divide.

Transubstantiation might seem to present a more formidable problem. As Schillebeeckx says, the Council of Trent deliberately used the doctrine of transubstantiation in order to pinpoint their disagreement with the Reformers.[11] But ever since Vatican II Roman Catholic theologians have been attempting to express the nature of Christ's presence in the eucharist in terms which are more comprehensible to modern intellects. Transubstantiation, at least as explained by Thomas Aquinas, 'has lost its significance in our times . . . It has lost its function as a banner because it can now be used to fly over ships with different cargoes' (to quote the same passage from Schillebeeckx). Schillebeeckx himself elaborates a theory which could perhaps be best described as 'transignification'. He begins from the position of a modern Swiss Reformed scholar, Leenhardt: a thing is really what God intends it to be. Our faith can apprehend what God intends a thing to be. God intends the bread and wine to be the body and blood of Christ in the eucharist. Faith therefore apprehends God's true intention. For unfaith the elements are just bread and wine. This, says Schillebeeckx, is not sufficient for the Catholic: things are what God intends them to be 'in an absolute and inward manner'. The sacraments themselves, he adds, 'are interpersonal encounters between the believer and Christ'. He refers to Thomas Aquinas' dictum 'that the saving power of this sacrament is ultimately situated in the real presence of Christ in the believing community itself'. The eucharist is the sacramental form of Christ's giving himself; the elements signify and make real Christ himself. The gift is offered whether we accept it or not, but the real presence is only completely realised when faith accepts it. One might not unfairly sum up Schillebeeckx's position by saying that transignification expresses how we see it; transubstantiation expresses what really happens.[12]

Much the same teaching meets us from Karl Rahner, though he does not go as far as Schillebeeckx does in trying to elaborate an alternative account to that of transubstantiation. He writes: 'the word of the sacrament of the altar . . . is

supported by the faith of the Church which hears this word
and so confers on it its true reality, that of the powerfully
triumphant word'. Karl Rahner seems to confine this word to
the traditional 'words of consecration', but modern liturgical
research would suggest that we should think of the whole
thanksgiving prayer as effecting that consecration, rather than
the 'words of consecration' alone. However Rahner explains
transubstantiation thus: *substance* is what something really is;
species is what it appears to be. We must therefore understand
that in the deepest sense the *substance* of the consecrated bread
is Christ's body, since he has said so, the species remaining
unaltered. Ordinary bread is not this. He writes: 'the doctrine
of transubstantiation tells us no more than do the words of
Christ when I take them seriously. The function of this
doctrine is not to explain the real presence by accounting for
how takes place.' He adds that the sacramental presence is the
sign and means of the permanent presence of Christ in the
believer; and that the first must not be subordinated to the
second.[13]

What has happened is that Roman Catholics have not
abandoned the doctrine of transubstantiation, but that they are
now explaining it in terms which would be acceptable to a very
wide range of Christians, extending far beyond the boundaries
of the Roman Catholic Church. This is reflected in the Agreed
Statement of 1973 already referred to. In that agreement
transubstantiation is only mentioned in a footnote, where we
are told that in the Roman Catholic Church transubstantiation
is meant to affirm 'the fact of Christ's presence and of the
mysterious and radical change that takes place. In
contemporary Roman Catholic theology it is not understood
as explaining *how* the change takes place.' Since this Agreed
Statement marks such a significant step forward, we should
quote it at greater length:

> The real presence of his body and blood can, however, only
> be understood within the context of the redemptive activity
> whereby he gives himself, and in himself reconciliation,
> peace, and life to his own. . . . Through faith Christ's
> presence—which does not depend on the individual's faith

in order to be the Lord's real gift of himself to his
Church—becomes no longer just a presence for the believer,
but also a presence *with* him . . . . The elements are not mere
signs; Christ's body and blood become really present and
are really given'.

The Statement adds that through the consecratory prayer
(which it also calls 'a prayer of thanksgiving') the bread and
wine become the body and blood of Christ by the action of
the Holy Spirit.[14]

Even more impressive is the joint Roman Catholic–Lutheran
statement already referred to, which uses three adjectives to
describe Christ's presence in the eucharist: 'sacramental,
supernatural, and spiritual', and in which Lutherans confess
that transubstantiation as explained by modern Roman
Catholics is 'a legitimate way of trying to explain the mystery'.
Both sides conclude that 'we are no longer able to regard
ourselves as divided in the one holy catholic and apostolic
faith on these two points' that is, sacrifice and presence.[15]

This gratifying resolution of theological issues has been
brought about by an abandonment of Aristotelian
metaphysical categories on the part of Roman Catholics and a
realisation on the part of Protestants that the early eucharist
was a great deal more corporate and realistic than their own
Reformed liturgies would suggest. We must now turn to the
area of liturgy itself.

We ought to be able to state with some clarity what the
eucharist is, what it is intended to be in the Church, and
proceed on the strength of that to examine the shape which it
ought to take. The eucharist then, we may say, is the public
service of worship wherein the people of God gives thanks to
God for his act of salvation in Christ, offers itself in Christ to
the Father by virtue of Christ's one offering upon the cross,
makes a memorial of Christ's life, death, and resurrection by
means of the bread and wine which he has appointed, and
encounters his presence by the same means in communion. He
is present to his faithful people in the Holy Spirit by the means
of the bread and wine which in the process of the thanksgiving
become the effective signs of his presence. The eucharist is at

one and the same time an act of thanksgiving and offering, a structured liturgy and a banquet.[16] It should be marked by joy and the dignity proper to the main and central act of the Church's worship. It is the people's service, not exclusively that of the celebrant. We may heartily endorse the statement of a fine Scottish theologian: 'But it is not really individual ministers who celebrate sacraments; it is the whole Church in its corporate capacity as a royal priesthood bringing its offering through Christ to God.'[17]

The eucharistic revival has meant that today many parts of the Church are actually proposing as a model for normal Sunday worship a popular eucharist at which all the faithful are urged to communicate. Before endorsing this ideal (which we do), we should perhaps pause to consider the radical nature of this proposal. We are in fact asking the Church as a whole to go back on something like 1600 years of practice and revert to the eucharistic pattern of about the fourth century. The practice of weekly communion for the majority of the faithful obviously has dangers: the most obvious one is that the sacrament should fall into contempt through familiarity; that people should come to communion unprepared or with known and unforgiven sins on their conscience; that they should incur the penalty to which Paul refers in 1 Cor. 11.27–30 (quoted above, p. 59). It was largely because of this fear that the falling-off in Sunday communions took place from the fourth century onwards. It was because of this that the custom grew up of fasting communion, and later on the requirement that confession to a priest should precede communion. We must not underestimate these dangers, but there seem to be only two alternative practices to this one, non-communicating attendance for most of the laity most of the year, or occasional celebration of the eucharist on those times when the laity will communicate, and a non-eucharistic service as a substitute for normal Sunday worship. Of these three only the first can be justified on scriptural and theological grounds (there is no evidence in the New Testament for non-communicating attendance). No practice is without its attendant dangers. In a post–Constantinian era, a pre-Constantinian practice may well be the best.

Since Vatican II the Roman Catholic Church has radically altered its mode of celebrating the eucharist. The old Latin mass has been superseded in most countries by a translation into the vernacular; the shape of the mass itself has been modified so as to conform more closely to a primitive model. The faithful are now encouraged to communicate much more frequently than before, often weekly, and also to take a full part in the spoken (or sung) part of the service; rules about fasting and confession have been relaxed, ignored, or abolished. Universal communion in both kinds is not yet established, but may well be on the way. Very often the altar has been moved from the east wall of the church and so placed that the celebrant can stand behind it facing westwards. In certain circumstances it is now made quite legitimate for laity to assist in the administration of the elements at communion. It can be said without exaggeration that the Roman Catholic Church in little over a decade has carried through a reformation of its eucharistic practice that meets almost every one of the demands of the Reformers and has produced a eucharistic rite infinitely more satisfactory than that produced by any reformed Church in the sixteenth century.

The result is that we can now compile an outline of the eucharist which could be accepted by any informed Christian in the West as adequate and satisfying, no matter what his denominational allegiance. We propose therefore to suggest first such an outline in order to provide ourselves with a satisfactory criterion by which to judge the eucharistic rites of the Church of England. The order will of course fall into two main parts: the service of the word and the thanksgiving prayer. We need not draw up a list of the various parts of the service of the word, they will be constant no matter what the denominational tradition is: the faithful will wish to hear the Scriptures read, preferably from Old Testament, epistle, and gospel. There will be a sermon no doubt, probably followed by the recitation of the Creed. There should be a period of intercession, and Christians of the Reformation at least will look for a form of confession and absolution (though the primitive Church apparently did without this). The order will then continue as follows:

1. *Offertory*: here both the alms and the bread and wine to be used can be brought up and offered. This is a primitive feature, and it gives an opportunity for the congregation to associate themselves with the sanctification of work. It is not a moment of great theological significance, but it is certainly a most appropriate way of marking the transition from the service of the word to the thanksgiving.

2. *Thanksgiving Prayer*: this is the central core of the spoken part of the rite. It should be regarded as being itself the consecratory prayer, and should not be divided into (a) thanksgiving; (b) consecration. It is the thanksgiving that consecrates. It should include thanksgiving to God for all his mighty acts in Christ, creation, incarnation, cross and resurrection and gift of the Holy Spirit. It will inevitably contain a reference to the Last Supper and a rehearsal of the words of institution, but these should not be isolated so as to become a separable 'formula of consecration'. It should look forward as well as backwards and contain a reference to the eschatological aspect of the eucharist as an anticipation of the heavenly feast. The prayer should be so expressed that we not only give thanks for a past redemption but also make the memorial of that redemption and so enter into it ourselves or associate ourselves with it.

3. *Offering and Epiclesis*: there should be a section in which the Church, as represented by the worshipping congregation, offers itself in Christ to God. This is the very minimum that should be done. In some rites this offering is placed after the communion, but it would seem more appropriate if it comes before the communion in close proximity to the prayer in which we make the memorial of Christ's one offering. A very ancient tradition, traceable back into the second century, is that we offer the bread and the wine as a symbol of our self-offering (hence Augustine's statement that it is ourselves whom we see upon the altar). This has alarmed Protestants, who see it as moving too close to offering Christ and thereby falling into the mediaeval error of believing that in the mass we repeat Christ's sacrifice. But this is no necessary implication and Anglicans at any rate should have no objection if this is a feature of the prayer part of the rite. The *Epiclesis* originally

meant the invocation of the Holy Spirit upon the elements so that they become the body and blood of our Lord. As we have observed on p. 65, this is an essential feature of the service according to Eastern Orthodox theology. It is not apparently a very early feature, and we should not insist on a formal invocation of the Holy Spirit on the elements. But we would do well to require a reference to the Spirit in this context. The Holy Spirit is the means by which Christ is present with his people since his resurrection, and this is as true of the eucharist as of any other situation. Such a reference will also afford some protection against magical or automatic views of the eucharistic presence.

4. *Communion of the People*: except that it ought in normal circumstances to be communion in both kinds, we should not seek to make any other conditions about how communion is administered. This is the climax of the rite and should ideally include everyone. Certainly non-communicating attendance, despite the centuries of tradition which support it, is not to be encouraged as a general rule for the laity. This is the one salient point where we must differ from our brethren of the Orthodox Church. Admirable though their eucharistic worship is in many respects as compared with ours, here they cannot be defended. The service will of course conclude with a blessing or dismissal, but nothing of importance need (or perhaps should) come after the communion.

We now accordingly apply these criteria to the three orders for the eucharist which are authorised in the Church of England. I omit consideration of Series 1, since it is still based in its structure on the 1662 rite. Our standards are primarily theological, but they cannot be divorced from liturgical implications.

THE BOOK OF COMMON PRAYER OF 1662

The Prayer for the Church Militant comes after the offertory, thus tending to perpetuate a confusion that had crept into the Latin mass, whereby the intercessions appeared in the canon or thanksgiving section. This has little to be said for it. But a much more serious defect is that there is nothing in the *Book of Common Prayer* service which exactly corresponds to the great thanksgiving prayer of the primitive rite. We do indeed seem to begin a thanksgiving prayer with 'Lift up your hearts', but it only continues as far as the *Ter Sanctus*, the angelic hymn of praise, and ends without any reference to God's mighty acts in Christ. It is then abruptly interpolated with the Prayer of Humble Access. This is a beautiful prayer in itself, but is disastrous in this position, since our minds are diverted from giving thanks for what God has done to an expression of our sinfulness. When this is finished we do not resume a thanksgiving prayer. On the contrary we have what is often called the consecration prayer, though if we examine it closely we find that it does not actually claim to consecrate anything; it merely prays that by reception of the bread and wine we may be partakers of Christ's body and blood, and then rehearses the words of institution. However it has been used as a consecration prayer certainly and we may legitimately treat it as such. As a consecration prayer it is most unhappily isolated. No one reading the Prayer Book rite would ever guess that the thanksgiving consecrates; quite the reverse: the consecration is apparently effected by the formula of the words of institution, entirely in the mediaeval tradition. Moreover there is no mention of anything but the death of Christ as effecting our salvation; no word of creation, resurrection, ascension, or giving of the Spirit. Cranmer has in fact adopted a strictly Anselmic doctrine of the atonement, whereby it was the death of Christ isolated from his life which paid satisfaction to the Father. Two other marked defects in the rite must be pointed out: there is no mention whatever of the Holy Spirit until the prayers after communion, when he is joined with the Father and the Son in the conventional Trinitarian ascription at the end. Secondly the self-offering of the Church comes after the communion and even occurs only in an alternative prayer. We should however note that that prayer had the merit of mentioning the self-offering of the whole Church, a feature whose absence from the two other rites we may rightly deplore. We may add as a final criticism that the Prayer Book service is on the whole a sombre ceremony: the note of joy is rarely heard.

We must therefore conclude that by modern informed

eucharistic criteria the *BCP* is appallingly deficient. This does not mean that God has not used it as a means of eucharistic grace to countless generations of worshippers and uses it still. Indeed the haunting beauty of Cranmer's language has probably been responsible for our willingness to accept his sometimes very unsatisfactory theology. Series 1, which owes much to the revision of 1928, attempted to remedy some of the deficiencies of the 1662 rite. But we should not treat the *BCP* as the sum of all wisdom or a final theological authority for all time. Cranmer when he compiled this rite knew much less about early Christian worship than we do today; and his atonement theology was unduly influenced by Anselm. We must not be inhibited today by the restrictions inevitable in the sixteenth century in England.

SERIES 2

The compilers of Series 2 were obviously determined to restore the thanksgiving prayer to its primitive position (a movement common to all modern eucharistic rites whatever the tradition concerned); and this they have certainly done. The intercessions are back in their proper place, which is in the service of the word, and the thanksgiving prayer is allowed to proceed without the interruption of the Prayer of Humble Access, which now goes with the penitential material in the first part. The thanksgiving prayer itself also makes mention of all the great acts of God in Christ: creation, incarnation, passion, resurrection, ascension, and gift of the Spirit. The narrative of the institution is rightly encapsulated within the thanksgiving prayer, which ends with the memorial of God's redemption in Christ and a petition for worthy reception. We miss any association of the Holy Spirit with the eucharistic presence of Christ. The Spirit is only mentioned in connection with the acts of God to be remembered. And the provision for the self-offering of the Church strikes one as inadequate. It occurs only in an alternative prayer after communion and has no mention of the Church as such. One might also question the propriety of the *Agnus Dei* (admittedly only as one option) between the thanksgiving prayer and communion. Is this a suitable place to be reminded of one's sins? Nevertheless we must say that theologically and liturgically Series 2 is an immense improvement on the *BCP*.

SERIES 3

Series 3 is a revision of Series 2, not a new rite, as Series 2 was in relation to the *BCP* service. The only points of significant difference between Series 3 and Series 2 occur in the thanksgiving part; and where Series 3 differs from Series 2 it is usually for the better. Thus there is an *Epiclesis* in Series 3's thanksgiving prayer. After the *Ter Sanctus*, in the prayer which includes the narrative of the institution, the president prays 'grant that by the power of your Spirit these gifts of bread and wine may be to us his body and his blood'. Likewise at the very end of the thanksgiving prayer we have the petition 'renew us by your Spirit'. The note of joy is also even more in evidence here than it is in Series 2 (and Series 2 itself has far more joy in it than has the *BCP*); particularly pleasing is the response of the congregation to the narrative of the institution: 'Christ has died: Christ is risen: Christ will come again'; and the long prayer is ended not with a bare 'Amen' but with a response of blessing from Rev. 7.12. It is worth noting that Series 3 does not prescribe any 'manual acts' to accompany the 'words of institution' of the thanksgiving prayer. This is no doubt done with the admirable intention of emphasising that it is the whole thanksgiving that consecrates and not only one formula, 'this is my body' etc. At the same time it would probably be better to perform the 'manual acts' in order to show that in the eucharist we are doing something, not merely saying something or thinking something. The offering of ourselves takes place (no longer only optionally now) after the communion, and the Church is not mentioned in this context. But despite these minor defects we must judge that of all the three eucharistic rites permissible in the Church of England Series 3 is, from the point of view of theology, the best.

There is indeed a remarkable contrast between baptism and the eucharist in the contemporary practice of the Church. About baptism there is much division of opinion, much dissatisfaction with present practice among those best entitled to judge, a widespread opinion that a hard battle has to be fought before baptism can be restored to its proper place in the Church. About the eucharist on the other hand there is a great and growing consensus of opinion, a definite agreement as to what its structure should be (however varied be the actual traditions of its administration), a striking concord about its essential meaning, and an increasing tendency to give it in its reformed shape the central place in Christian worship. Whereas baptism to some extent divides us, the eucharist unites us. For this growing unity on the central subject of the eucharist we should be most thankful. It provides us with one of our brightest hopes for the future.

5 The ministry in history

THE obvious starting-point for an historical consideration of the Christian ministry is the twelve apostles. What did Jesus intend them to be and what was their relation to their successors? All three Synoptic Gospels agree that Jesus chose twelve special disciples. It is not at all certain that he gave them the name of 'apostles' (or its Aramaic equivalent). The phrase in Mark 3.14 'whom also he named apostles' is absent from a number of important manuscripts and is relegated to the margin of the *RSV*. It is Luke who emphasises that Jesus called them apostles. Matthew only uses the word once (Matt. 10.2) and Mark only once elsewhere (Mark 6.30.). John pointedly refrains from using the word as a title. For him the Son is the apostle *par excellence*. All four evangelists prefer the term 'the Twelve'. The actual term 'apostle' may therefore reflect the mind of the early Church.

However the word undoubtedly describes the status of the Twelve: they were the special representatives of Jesus, who is the special representative of God. The fact that they were twelve in number is significant: they were to be the nucleus of faithful Israel in the end-time. But can we say more than that? Were they also to be officers or princes of faithful Israel, the Christian Church? This is the traditional view, and is defended by all those who believe that Jesus instituted the ministry of the Church in the persons of the apostles. Certainly some evidence from the New Testament can be cited in favour of this view: in Matt. 16.18–19 and 18.18, as we have already observed, Jesus seems to be handing over authority to Peter and to the disciples. Again in John 20.22–3 the disciples seem to be granted authority in the words: 'If you forgive the sins of any, they are forgiven; if you retain the sins of any, they are retained.' Similarly the charge in Matt. 28.19–20 to make disciples of all nations and baptise them seems to be an empowering of the Eleven. Clearest of all is the little parable in Luke 12.42–43: 'Blessed is that servant whom his master when he comes will find so doing . . . etc.': this seems to demand a situation where some are in command and some under authority within the household of faith. Nor must we ignore the obvious fact that we have a description in Acts of the early Church in Jerusalem in which the apostles hold authority with the elders under them, and with James the brother of the Lord apparently holding a pre-eminent position among the apostles. We could also quote the two passages in Luke 22.29–30 and Matt. 19.28 where the Twelve are to sit on thrones judging the tribes of Israel.

In this material however we must distinguish passages which give the Twelve authority generally from those which suggest that they have authority over the members of the Church. They receive authority to loose and bind and to forgive sins, not perhaps because they are officers of the new Israel, but because they are the nucleus of the new Israel. Thus a passage such as Luke 22.29f. makes best sense if seen as a promise that as faithful Israel they will judge unfaithful Israel; it is coupled with the promise: 'you shall eat and drink at my table in my kingdom' which surely applies to all of faithful Israel. Similarly the passage in John 20.21f. seems to be a giving of authority to the Church as a whole, not to officers of the Church. Most scholars agree that John was not concerned with the ministry of the Church. The same may well be true of Matt. 28.18f.: it is the whole Church that has the duty of proclaiming the gospel and baptising. I would suggest that the reason why the apostles are so prominent in the early chapters of Acts is that at first they were the new Israel *in nucleo*. As the book proceeds they seem to fade out, because Acts is the story of how the original disciples broadened out into a Church of Jew and Gentile far beyond the borders of Palestine. By the end of Acts the Church is no longer ruled by the Twelve. We are left with the parable of the household in Luke 12.42f. (and Matt. 24.42f.). In its original context I would be inclined to class it with such parables as that of the Talents or the Wise and Foolish Virgins; he who makes best use of his time and gifts will receive his reward in the kingdom.[1]

The famous Petrine promise in Matt. 16.16–20 is certainly meant by the author of the First Gospel to signify that Peter is given special authority in the Church. As we have already observed, the passage is not in itself sufficient basis for the claims in connection with the authority of the Bishop of Rome which were later made. It requires further evidence to show that the promise extends to Peter's successors, and to link Peter with the see of Rome. The most obvious interpretation would seem to be that Peter is, so to speak, the Abraham of the new Israel, the proto-believer. The Church is to be built on faith in Jesus as the Messiah. This does not in itself suggest jurisdiction. In any case it would be rash to build too much on the historicity of Matthew's addition to Mark's account of the Caesarea Philippi episode.

When we turn to the evidence supplied by Paul, the significance of the apostles seems by no means easy to assess. Paul never refers to the Twelve unambiguously as 'the apostles'. The nearest he gets to it is in Gal. 1.17–19, where he writes: 'nor did I go up to Jerusalem to those who were apostles before me'. But it is very difficult to resist the conclusion that this group includes James the brother of the Lord, who was not one of the Twelve. Paul refers to 'the Twelve' only once, in 1 Cor. 15.5 in connection with their function as witnesses of the resurrection. In 15.7 he seems to imply that 'all the apostles' and 'the Twelve' are not synonymous terms. He also uses the word 'apostle' for himself frequently and emphatically, and in 2 Corinthians in particular he seems to be asserting his right to the name against those who are denying it. He describes these people as 'these superlative apostles' (2 Cor. 11.5; 12.11) and 'false apostles' (11.13). Unless we are to adopt the very unwelcome conclusion that Paul is here directly referring to the Twelve, we must assume that his detractors claimed to be apostles themselves (however illegitimately); in which case the term 'apostle' could not possibly be confined to some sort of a 'college' of Twelve or more. Paul also uses the term apostle for others besides himself and the apostles at Jerusalem: in 1 Thess. 2.7 he applies the word apparently to himself, Silvanus, and Timothy. In 1 Cor. 4.9 he probably includes Apollos with himself under the term 'us apostles'; and 9.4–6 surely implies that he regards Barnabas as an apostle. But the ring of apostles extends even wider: in Rom. 16.7 two individuals of whom we know absolutely nothing are described as 'men of note among the apostles'. They could not possibly have belonged to the original Twelve, or Twelve plus certain special individuals such as Paul himself. We also have in 2 Cor. 8.23 a group called 'apostles of the churches'. Many scholars say the term is used in a non-technical sense here to mean simply 'messenger'; but in Phil. 2.25 Epaphroditus, who had been apparently carrying out very similar work to that of Silvanus, Timothy, and Barnabas, is called 'your apostle'. It may well be that the term carries its full evangelistic sense both here and in 2 Cor. 8.23.

The impression we gain from Paul is that he uses the word 'apostle' to mean anyone who had been commissioned to carry out evangelistic work, and not to apply only to the members of a limited 'college'. The apostle had authority over the churches which he had evangelised, though not apparently beyond them (see Rom. 1.11–12; 15.20–21; 2 Cor. 10.15–16).

This conclusion is scouted by those who believe that there was a limited apostolic college which received Christ's authority and handed it on to duly appointed successors. They would distinguish two senses for the word 'apostle': (a) for the Twelve plus certain other specific individuals; (b) a non-technical sense applicable to everyone who undertook evangelistic work. The difficulty lies in determining the 'plus'. We allow Paul of course (but when was he commissioned?) and Barnabas and certainly James the Lord's brother. Others would seem to have an equally strong claim: Silvanus, for example. The more you put into the 'plus', the more difficult it becomes to decide what were the qualifications or method of entry for the apostolic college.

But the really insuperable difficulty in this theory of an apostolic college that passed on its authority to successors lies in showing when, where, or to whom they passed their authority. We have simply no record of anyone who can by the loosest definition be termed an apostle handing on his apostolic authority to anyone else. The only apostle of whom we have any certain or continuous knowledge is Paul; we never find him engaged in the act of ordaining anyone, though there is some evidence that he set up some sort of a local ministry in the Churches which he founded, and he and Barnabas are represented as doing so in Acts 14.23. In 1 Cor. 16.15f. Stephanas, a first convert, seems to hold a position of authority; compare also 1 Thess. 5.12–13. In Phil. 1.1 we have a greeting addressed to 'all the saints in Christ Jesus who are at Philippi, with the bishops and deacons'. This is the only use of *episkopos* (bishop) in the Pauline letters and must mean the local group of ministers.[2] 'Deacon' does not seem yet to be a technical term and appears to mean simply 'workers'. Paul never uses the term 'presbyter' for the local ministry. This term appears in Acts, where the 'presbyters' seem to hold a rank subordinate to the apostles. It seems very likely that the term was borrowed from the 'elders' of the Jewish synagogue. Perhaps the bishops (*episkopoi*) in a Pauline church corresponded to the presbyters in the Church at Jerusalem. That the two terms ultimately coincided we may be sure. Thus it seems likely that Paul entrusted the organisation of the local Church to a group of local ministers. But this is not at all the same thing as giving them apostolic authority. We have no record of any other original apostle handing on his authority to anyone. The apostolic function, to be the nucleus of the new Israel and to witness to the Lord's resurrection, seems to have been entrusted to the Church as a whole. We have no record of any original dominical authority being passed on from the original apostles to any group of ministers.

Paul does however have a doctrine of the ministry. It is so unlike what we demand from a New Testament doctrine of the ministry (accreditation of our own ministry and guidelines for judging other ministries), that we normally fail to perceive it. But it is there. We must begin by remarking that according to Paul's doctrine the mixed Jewish–Gentile Church of his day, as the faithful remnant in the days of the Messiah, has taken the place of Israel of old in God's design, and now has the duty and privilege of preaching the gospel to the whole world. This is argued out in great detail in Rom. 9–11. The argument is much too elaborate to be reproduced here, but we should notice that the faithful remnant certainly has the task of proclaiming the gospel. See Rom. 10.14–15: 'But how are men to call upon him in whom they have not believed? And how are they to believe in him of whom they have never heard? And how are they to hear without a preacher? And how can men preach unless they are sent?' Thus the faithful remnant of first believers in Jesus as Lord, as it broadens out into the Jewish–Gentile Church of Paul's mature experience, has the duty of preaching the gospel, passing on the knowledge of Christ to those who do not know him.

But Paul is more specific than this: in some passages of his letters he represents himself and his fellow-workers as actually re-enacting or representing the life of Christ in the Churches which they have founded. Consider for example 1 Cor. 4.9f.:

> For I think that God has exhibited us apostles as last of all, like men sentenced to death; because we have become a spectacle to the world, to angels and to men. We are fools for Christ's sake, but you are wise in Christ. We are weak, but you are strong. You are held in honour, but we in disrepute. To the present hour we hunger and thirst, we are ill-clad and buffeted and homeless, and we labour, working with our own hands. When reviled, we bless; when persecuted, we endure; when slandered, we try to conciliate; we have become, and are now, as the refuse of the world, the offscouring of all things.

We cannot avoid noticing in this passage the way in which the life of the ministers (Paul and his companions) is described in terms just as appropriate to the life of Christ. In particular those two words translated 'refuse' and 'offscouring' have an atoning, expiatory significance in the Greek. Similar passages occur in 2 Cor. 4.7–15 and 6.3–10. We have then in Paul the conception of a ministerial task with which those are charged who preach the gospel and found and care for Churches. It is nothing less than to live out the life of Christ in the Churches they found. The emphasis is all on humble service (though this is not inconsistent with quite sharp discipline, as all Paul's

letters witness). And the whole activity is undertaken in order
to enable the Church as a whole to live the life of Christ. This
is not therefore a vicarious ministry, nor is it an autocratic
ministry responsible only to itself. It is apostolic, energising,
sacramental, eschatological. By it the very life, death, and
resurrection of Christ is passed on to the Church. Thus we
have in Paul the outline of a doctrine of the ministry which is
very unlike any traditional account of the ministry; it is
profoundly related to the servant status of the Lord and thus to
the incarnation. It does not answer any of our traditional
questions, but puts a number of disturbing questions to us.

But there is in the New Testament a deep strand of teaching
which underlies indeed Paul's doctrine of the ministry. This is
diakonia or service. It goes back to the profound conception of
the Lord as the servant of his people, so clearly expressed in
Mark 10.45: 'For the Son of man also came not to be served
but to serve [the verb is *diakonein*], and to give his life as a
ransom for many.' *Diakonia* implies subordinate service,
though not necessarily slavery. It can be used of specifically
Christian pastoral ministry, as in Acts 1.17; Rom. 11.13; or of
some particular service, as for example Paul's great scheme of
bringing famine relief to the Christians in Judaea (Rom.
15.31). It can refer to the entire ministry of a local Church, as
in Rev. 2.19; and of the universal Church, as in Eph. 4.12. The
noun *diakonos* is used of Christ directly in Rom. 15.8: 'Christ
became a servant to the circumcised' and by implication of
course in Mark 10.45. In John 12.26 it seems to refer to all
faithful Christians. Paul frequently uses the word of himself
and his companions: 1 Cor. 3.5; 2 Cor. 3.6; 11.23; Col. 1.7,23;
4.7.

Thus ministry in the New Testament is neither exclusively
liturgical nor exclusively clerical. It is thoroughly secular (in
the sense that it goes on in the market place) and thoroughly
ecclesial (in the sense that it is an activity of the Church). The
whole thing is beautifully summed up in Eph. 4.12. The author
of the epistle has been explaining how God gives gifts to the
Church in the form of various types of ministry. Then he
explains in verse 12 what the purpose of this ministry is: 'to
equip God's people for work in his service'.[3] In other words,

the purpose of the special ministry is to enable the Church to carry out its ministry, which is in fact Christ's ministry.

Most of those who look for an account of the ordained ministry in the New Testament turn to 1 Cor. 12.28 and Eph. 4.11, because in both these passages we seem to have a list of orders in the ministry. But the notion of a graded hierarchy of ordained ministers is quite foreign to Paul and equally foreign is our modern clericalised notion that only the ordained ministry could be expected to do the Church's work. What Paul (or his disciple) is doing in both these passages is giving a list of the actual gifts possessed and exercised by Christians, and urging that they are given for the good of the Church, not the gratification of the possessor. With the exception of apostleship any name in either list may equally apply to someone who is a minister and someone who is not. The question of whether you are ordained or not does not affect the sort of gift you have.

The same remark applies to the *charismata* or spiritual gifts which the Corinthians so much admired. Possessing a *charisma* was not incompatible with being a minister, nor was a *charisma* inoperative except in an ordained minister. *Diakonia* or service was the duty of all and some might have the particular *diakonia* of pastoral oversight. The same view is found in 1 Pet. 4.10: 'As each has received a gift [*charisma*], employ it for one another ['employ' is *diakonein*], as good stewards of God's varied grace'. All are to engage in ministry; anyone might have a *charisma*. But the author of 1 Peter certainly knew of a local ordained ministry; see 5.1–5. This letter probably belongs to a time at least a generation later than Paul. But the doctrine of the ministry is the same.

There has been much debate as to the meaning of the word *episkopos* (? bishop) in the New Testament. In pagan usage it could mean anything from a temple trustee to an inspector of drains. It is unlikely that there is any direct connection with the *mebaqqer* of the Qumran community. Outside the Pastoral Epistles (which we discuss below) the word only occurs in Phil. 1.1; Acts 20.28; and 1 Pet. 2.25 (where it applies to Christ). In the Acts passage it is impossible to deny that 'presbyters' and 'bishops' are synonymous terms. In Phil. 1.1 the *episkopoi* must mean the local group of pastors in charge. The word, like *diakonos*, was borrowed from pagan usage and applied first to the local ministry as a simple alternative to 'presbyter'.

This leads naturally on to the question of priesthood in the New Testament. Christ is the priest *par excellence*, though the name is only explicitly applied to him in Hebrews. The name is never applied to any Christian minister in the New Testament, just as no word taken from the Old Testament cult is applied. But Christians as a whole are called priests in Rev. 1.6; 5.10; 20.6; and in 1 Pet. 2.3–9 we have the classic description of Christian priesthood. We quote verse 5: 'and like living stones be yourselves built into a spiritual house, to be a holy priesthood, to offer spiritual sacrifices acceptable to God through Jesus Christ'. Note that this is a corporate priesthood, it belongs to the Church. If we want a description of these 'spiritual sacrifices', we can turn back to Rom. 12.1: 'present your bodies as a living sacrifice, holy and acceptable to God, which is your spiritual worship'. The Church's sacrifice is the offering of itself in Christ. This is in fact the Christian life, even though it is described in terms of worship.

Does this mean then that Christian worship is wholly desacralised; to be carried out in the market place and not in temples? No, because the primary Christian duty is thanksgiving; indeed this very point is made in 1 Pet. 2.9, where the task of the 'royal priesthood' is 'to declare the wonderful deeds of him who called you out of darkness into his marvellous light'. This helps to explain why, as we have seen, thanksgiving (precisely declaring God's wonderful acts in Christ) is the central theme of the early Christian eucharist. It provides an essential link between worship, faith, and life.

But we must not conclude that there is no justification in the New Testament for a derived or representative priesthood of ordained ministers. It can, however, only come through the priesthood of the Church. We have in the New Testament the ministry (*diakonia*) of the whole Church, received from Christ through the apostles. In order that the Church may exercise this *diakonia* effectively, it must commission a special order of ministers, who are called *diakonoi*; we see this order emerging during the period covered by the New Testament. But the ministers are not vicars or surrogates for Christ; they are representatives of the Church, and hence of Christ. Because the Church possesses Christ's authority, they also possess it. But this is not a worldly authority (though Paul could exercise it quite severely). It bears the paradoxical mark of Christ's authority, that is, it is shown in serving, in self-effacement, and in suffering for those over whom it is exercised. Thus, if we are asked to describe the doctrine of the ministry to be found in the New Testament, we must say that it is neither the executive, vicarious, clericalised ministry of traditional Catholicism; nor is it the advisory, egalitarian, democratic ministry of modern Protestantism. It is a representative priesthood, bearing the authority of Christ in the Church and for the Church, whose authenticity can only be proved in service and suffering.

I take the Pastoral Epistles to have been written at the very end of the first century by a Church leader who wished to maintain Paul's tradition, but had only the flimsiest direct links with Paul. In his time no doubt ordination to the presbyterate was by the laying-on of hands of the group of local presbyters (see 1 Tim. 4.14). The great question is, do the Pastorals witness to the existence of monepiscopacy? There is evidence on both sides; the most likely explanation is that the author was writing at a time when the government of the local Church by one *episkopos* assisted by a group of presbyters had emerged in Asia Minor, but was not prevalent everywhere by any means. The author is conscious that it had not emerged in Paul's time. There is in the Pastorals clear evidence for the existence of an order of deacons subordinate to the bishop or presbyters. There is no certain evidence for this earlier. The seven of Acts 6.1–6 are not called deacons and are not deacons in the later sense.

The date of the *Didache* is uncertain; many scholars would put it actually in the first century. Others would place it about AD 130, though conceding that it contains earlier material. In it there are only *episcopoi* and *diakonoi* and no trace of monepiscopacy. Despite strenuous efforts in the past to prove the contrary, there is no sign of monepiscopacy in the church of Rome when Clement wrote his epistle to the Church at Corinth about AD 96. His *episkopoi* are the group of local ministers; under them are the deacons. He produces a scriptural proof for the institution of the ministry, Isa. 60.17, but it depends for its point on a Greek translation of the Hebrew which is different from that found in the Septuagint. It looks as if he had discovered it for himself, since he would hardly have produced so unconvincing a proof had he known any tradition on the subject. On the other hand he does advance an argument which looks like the germ of the theory of apostolic succession. He writes as follows:

> Our Apostles knew also, through Our Lord Jesus Christ, that there would be strife over the dignity of the bishop's office. For this reason therefore, having received complete foreknowledge, they appointed the aforesaid [sc. *episkopoi* and *diakonoi* in each church], and after a time made provision that on their death other approved men should succeed in their ministry.[4]

Note that 'the bishop's office' here does not refer to monepiscopacy, but to the group of bishop-presbyters in each Church. It might be fair to say that here we have a doctrine of continuity from the apostles without the necessary implication of succession by ordination.

In Ignatius (*c.* 110) monepiscopacy emerges for the first time into the full light of day. Ignatius is an enthusiastic supporter of this system; so enthusiastic that we suspect it must be under attack. In every letter (except that to Rome, a significant exception) he mentions the bishop and frequently adds an exhortation to support and obey him. The bishop is often described as a type or representation of God, and Ignatius does not wish that anything important in the church (for example a eucharist or baptism) should take place without the bishop's presence or at least approval. But he emphasises the importance of the two other orders: presbyters and deacons, just as much. Where the bishop is compared to God or Christ, the presbyters are compared to the apostles. Nor are the laity ignored. In his Letter to Polycarp 6.1 he refers to the whole church in Smyrna as 'stewards, assessors, and ministers of God'. In Ignatius therefore we find the first sketch of a theology of the three-fold ministry. He does relate the ministry to God in Christ, and he does define the purpose of the ministry, to represent God in Christ to the contemporary Church. The Church as a whole reflects back God in Christ by its existence. This is a more static doctrine than Paul's, but within measurable distance of his.

There is one class of people in the New Testament who seemed likely at one time to form a distinct order on their own: the prophets. Paul gives a place to prophets high on his list (1 Cor. 12.28; Eph. 4.11). They appear often in Acts; in 1 Tim. 4.14 prophecy seems to accompany the appointment of ministers. There is a book of prophecy in the New Testament, the Revelation. Ignatius seems to have claimed the gift of prophecy. In the *Didache* prophets are more highly esteemed than the local ministers. It was the one order that could claim continuity with the Old Testament. Probably what killed it as a permanent feature of the Christian ministry was the rise of Montanism in the second century, a Pentecostal movement in which prophecy ran riot. But we should observe that up to about AD 150 there was nothing whatever discreditable in a member of the clergy claiming to be a prophet.

The doctrine of apostolic succession which we find tentatively sketched in Clement's letter was elaborated by later theologians. In Irenaeus (fl. 180–200) and Tertullian (fl. 200–220) the emphasis is more on succession in teaching than on succession in ordination, but gradually it came to be accepted that the apostles must have consciously instituted a successive ministry, and the major sees such as Rome, Antioch, and Alexandria began compiling succession lists of their bishops tracing their lineage back to an apostle or companion of the apostles.

In the doctrine of the ministry, as in the doctrine of the eucharist, Cyprian occupies an important place. We have seen how he was anxious to find a sacrifice for the Christian priest to offer as the Old Testament priest had offered his, and how he found it in the sacrifice of Christ's passion. This meant that from Cyprian's time onwards in the West there is a tendency to regard the Christian minister as primarily a sacrificing priest; his normative function is to offer the eucharistic sacrifice. In line with this Cyprian tried to find an equation between the priesthood of the new dispensation and that of the old. The equation he found was this: the Jewish high priest has been superseded by Christ the great High Priest; the Jewish priest corresponds to the Christian bishop; both presbyters and deacons correspond to the Jewish Levite. This might have been acceptable as a devotional analogy, but when it was taken literally it resulted in a dangerous influx of Old Testament ideas into the theology of the ministry. Thus the physical qualifications required of an Old Testament priest were applied to the Christian priesthood (he must be a male; he must not be physically disabled; he must not be impotent, etc.). As the dark ages closed round the Church the Christian priest began to look more and more like the ritually qualified hierophant of a pagan religion, and less like the figure whom Paul or even Ignatius present to us.

At the same time Cyprian tried to work out a theology of episcopacy as such: he regarded the bishop in his own diocese as the holder and arbiter of all Church authority; in his own diocese he is not subject to the control of any other bishop. 'What the bishop is to his own diocese—the guardian and symbol of unity—such is the college of bishops to the whole Church.'[5] Cyprian himself writes: 'The episcopate is one: each individual bishop holds a part in what is common to all bishops.'[6] There is doubt as to how far Cyprian acknowledged a primacy in the see of Rome on the basis of the promise made to Peter in Matt. 16.16f. Cyprian was no arbitrary tyrant, however; he always tried to consult his presbyters and people in matters of ordination. He habitually addressed his clergy as 'my fellow-presbyters'. He also frequently consulted his fellow-bishops in provincial synods, in which each bishop had one vote. But he did not regard the decisions made there as binding on individual bishops. In one point he is remarkable also: what decides whether a minister can validly administer the sacraments is not the worthiness of his character, nor a 'character' given him by virtue of ordination, but the regularity of his position in the Church. Thus an excommunicated minister *ipso facto* loses his orders. Anglicans have tended to appeal to the Cyprianic doctrine of the Church and ministry as a suitable ideal in contrast to the Roman Catholic doctrine of a

Church subordinate to the papacy. But Cyprian's doctrine taken in all strictness would hardly fit in with the present structures of Anglicanism.

The most striking development as far as the ministry is concerned during the Middle Ages was the rise of the power and claims of the papacy. As long as the Byzantine emperor held any power in the West there was a counterbalance to papal authority. When barbarian conquest interposed a barrier between the Eastern and the Western empires, the pope was left without an ecclesiastical rival. Later the papal claims were accentuated by the struggle with the Holy Roman Emperor, which found a sort of solution in 1122, when an agreement was reached between Calixtus II and the Emperor Henry V. From its peak under Innocent III in 1215, the political power of the popes waned during the thirteenth century, but their theoretical claims increased, reaching a climax in Boniface VIII's Bull *Unam Sanctam* in 1302, with its terrific claim: 'we declare, state, define, and pronounce that it is altogether necessary to salvation to every human creature to be subject to the Roman pontiff'. The exaltation of the pope tended, in theory at least, to weaken the position of the bishop. At times it almost seemed as if the Roman Catholic Church believed in three major orders: pope, bishop-presbyter, and deacon. Thomas Aquinas held that the episcopate is not a separate order in the sense in which order is a sacrament. This is because episcopal consecration adds nothing to the priest's power in the eucharist. But it is a separate order in the sense that 'in hierarchical actions (ordination, doctrine, government) a bishop has in relation to the mystical body a higher power than a priest'.

In the East the episcopate soon came under the power of the state. This prevented the growth of an eastern papacy, but also hindered any development in a Cyprianic direction. Even when the Byzantine Empire fell in 1454 the patriarchate in Constantinople continued to be under the direction of a Muslim government. In Russia a parallel patriarchate developed, but from the time of Peter the Great (early eighteenth century) the Church was increasingly treated as a department of state by the Tsarist government. When Tsarism fell in 1917, it was succeeded by a still more repressive régime, violently anti-religious and determined that religion should disappear. It has combined persecution and erastianism in a way that the Ottoman Turks might well have envied. The consequence is that Orthodoxy has never had much opportunity to show what it makes of episcopacy in a free society. It has however exhibited a pattern of autocephalous (independent) Churches in communion with each other which is reminiscent of the Anglican Communion and may well prove a useful example in future ecumenical developments.

All the Reformers were compelled to work out some sort of a theology of the ministry, since all of them organised or continued a Church in defiance of the Roman obedience. Luther, who had not originally intended to set up a new Church, found himself running out of ministers in the early 1520s; his first ordination was at Wittenberg in 1525. He reverted to the priesthood of all Christians conferred in baptism and he claimed that, where the constituted ministers had failed, the local Christian congregation by virtue of their baptismal priesthood could ordain ministers of the gospel. This argument has more force to it than might at first appear, since, as we have argued above, the priesthood of the ordained ministry does derive from the priesthood of the Church. The difficulty lies in deciding when such action is justified. Lutheranism has ever since tended to claim that matters of order are not fundamental, and that order is not constitutive of the Church. Any form of church order that is not contrary to the gospel is legitimate. Consequently we find in Lutheranism episcopal systems and presbyteral systems existing side by side. Swedish Lutheranism has actually preserved the episcopal succession in consecration from the pre-Reformation episcopate. But the Swedish Church freely recognises the orders of all Lutheran ministers, and makes no theological capital out of its preservation of the succession.

John Calvin went about matters in a very different way; he believed that he had rediscovered by his study of the New Testament the true form of ministry intended by Christ. He claimed that in Matt. 18.15-20 our Lord formally transferred jurisdiction from the Sanhedrin to the apostles as the first ministers of the Church. He also made much use of Eph. 4.1–

16 as the charter of the Church's ministry: he distinguishes two kinds of presbyter (or elder, or bishop); there is the ruling elder and the teaching elder. These have in fact in most Presbyterian Churches developed into the local minister (ruling elder) and his elders (teaching elder). Calvin identified the primitive monepiscopal bishop with the ruling elder and his presbyters with the teaching elders. He therefore had no objection whatever to primitive episcopacy and highly approved of both Ignatius and Cyprian. Thus in his doctrine of the ministry Calvin is really very 'catholic' in the sense that according to him the authority of the Church lies ultimately in the hands of the ministry and not of the laity. In practice however Reformed Churches have shown themselves to be pioneers in the democratic way of organising the Church and of integrating the laity into the government of the Church. Since many other Churches, Anglican and Episcopal included, are today attempting to reorganise their government on these lines, the Presbyterians have been our schoolmasters and we have much to learn from them.

The radical Reformers, Anabaptists, Mennonites, Congregationalists, and so on, tended to blur the line between ministry and laity and to insist (quite rightly of course) that ministry was the task of the whole Church. This meant both that laity were empowered to perform any duty in the Church, including celebrating the eucharist, and that the appointment of ministers came into the hands of the local congregation. In fact almost no body of Christians has attempted to dispense with a separate ministry altogether. The Society of Friends might seem to have done this, since they have no rites of ordination, but in fact this is not the case: their argument is that, if God has given an individual the gift of ministry, no human act can add anything to it. If God has not given it, no human act can give it. This is of course an individualist view of the ministry and hardly does justice to the very corporate doctrine which we find in the New Testament. But they do not deny that certain persons do have the gift of ministry.

The Church of England alone among the Churches of the Reformation deliberately continued the three orders which were maintained in the mediaeval Church, and the succession of consecration of bishops was maintained through the period of the break with Rome, the reign of Edward VI, the Marian reaction and the restoration of a Reformed polity under Elizabeth I. The first apologists for the Church of England, Jewel and Hooker, did not defend episcopacy as being of the essence of the Church. They were content to argue that episcopacy was not contrary to the word of God. Hooker himself believed it had been instituted by the apostles, was authorised by God, and was necessary for the perfection of the Church. But he refused to unchurch non-episcopal Churches such as the Church of Scotland and the Reformed Church in France. The Ordinal of the Church of England maintains (quite unhistorically) that the three orders have existed since the time of the apostles and requires that all ordained in the Church of England should be episcopally ordained, but makes no pronouncement about the position of non-episcopal Churches. This was roughly the position of the Church of England up to the beginning of the nineteenth century. For example when Archbishop Wake corresponded with the Swiss Reformed theologians about possible union in 1717 onwards, though he urged them to accept episcopacy, he never suggested that their ministers would need to be re-ordained or that they did not constitute genuine Churches at all.

The rise of the Oxford Movement, developing into the Anglo-Catholic party in the Church of England, changed all this. One of the great principles of the Tractarians, one which emboldened them to claim that the Church of England was independent of the state, was their belief in 'the apostolical succession'. We have already seen in Chapter 1 how this produced the Branch Theory of the Church. Thus the belief that the bishops of the Church of England could trace their descent by successive laying-on of hands of bishops back to the apostles became a fundamental tenet of Anglo-Catholic belief; and with it went the corollary that non-episcopal Churches had no valid orders, very doubtful sacraments, and could not be regarded as authentic Churches at all. Consequently from about 1850 onwards it has been impossible to obtain from any representative Anglican gathering anything like a recognition of non-episcopal orders in any circumstances; and it is Anglicans rather than Roman Catholics who have made the most strenuous efforts to prove the fact of apostolic succession on historical grounds. Even as recently as 1943 as well-informed an Anglican leader as William Temple could write as follows:

> The Apostles were in no sense ministers of the laity; they were ministers of Christ to the laity, and to the world waiting to be won. They took steps for the perpetuation of the ministry and it has descended to ourselves. So when I consecrate a godly and well-learned man to the office and work of a Bishop in the Church of God, I do not act as representative of the Church, if by that is meant the whole number of contemporary Christians; but I do act as the ministerial instrument of Christ in His Body the Church. The authority by which I act is His, transmitted to me through His apostles and those to whom they committed it; I hold it neither from the Church nor apart from the Church, but from Christ in the Church.[7]

After the Reformation the Roman Catholic Church clung resolutely to the mediaeval doctrine of priesthood, emphasising especially its sacrificial aspect. The dogma of the Infallibility of the Pope, proclaimed in 1870, seemed to eliminate for ever any hope that the Roman Catholic Church would allow room for any doctrine that made the ministry in any way responsible to the Church, for it defined the infallibility as follows:

> That the Roman Pontiff, when he speaks *ex cathedra* (that is, when—fulfilling the office of Pastor and Teacher of all Christians—on his supreme Apostolical authority, he defines a doctrine concerning faith and morals to be held by the Universal Church), through the divine assistance promised him in blessed Peter, is endowed with that infallibility, with which the Divine Redeemer has willed that His Church—in defining doctrine concerning faith or morals—should be equipped: And therefore, that such definitions of the Roman Pontiff in themselves—and not by virtue of the consent of the Church—are irreformable.[8]

The Roman Catholic Church would also seem to have taken a

further step towards complete divorce from the Church of England in the doctrine of the ministry when in 1896 Pope Leo XIII issued his Bull *Apostolicae Curae* on the subject of Anglican orders. He declared that the intention of the ordination rites of the Anglican Church is defective because there are no acts or words explicitly conferring upon priests the power to offer sacrifice. He therefore pronounced that 'ordinations performed according to the Anglican rite are utterly invalid and altogether void'. But despite these trenchant statements much has happened both in the Church of Rome and within Anglicanism since 1896. Even the most explicit formulae cannot bind later generations.

6 A theology of the ministry

As with the doctrine of the Church, so with the doctrine of the ministry, there have been developments during the twentieth century which have very considèrably loosened the apparently inflexible positions taken up by nineteenth-century theologians and have disclosed a possibility of *rapprochement* which would have seemed inconceivable to them. We may be content here to mention two such developments; the first in the realm of theory, the second in that of practice.

The first is this: it has become clear to the great majority of scholars that the traditional doctrine of the apostolic succession cannot be maintained on grounds of historical evidence. This is more than an admission that the traditional form in which it was presented is untenable. No one who knows anything about the subject would maintain today that Christ appointed the apostles to be rulers of the Church, the apostles appointed the first bishops, and since then the succession has been handed on unbroken by means of episcopal consecration to the modern episcopate. It is true that this view is explicitly contained in the Vatican II document *Lumen Gentium*, which says that Jesus Christ 'willed that their [that is, the apostles'] successors, namely the bishops, should be shepherds in the Church even to the consummation of the world':[1] but this document had to look both ways, back to traditional positions as well as forward to new formulations; and, as we shall be seeing, since then Roman Catholic scholars have spoken with much less dogmatism and more regard to historical evidence. No, what cannot now be maintained without adding doctrinal assumptions to historical evidence is that the apostles deliberately transmitted Church authority to anyone, or that one can trace any line of transmission of authority through ordained ministers from them to the first bishops, Ignatius of Antioch and his contemporaries. The last attempt to do this by means of producing historical evidence in a scholarly way was in the symposium edited by Kenneth Kirk, *The Apostolic Ministry*.[2] Eminent though the various contributions to this book were, and valiantly though they strove to produce arguments drawn from history, New Testament scholarship, and rabbinic literature to prove their case, we can say today with some confidence that they failed to prove that something somehow was transmitted from the apostles to the first bishops. This does not mean that the doctrine of apostolic succession is not held in the Church of England or elsewhere. It is held and still forms an important element in the thought of what today represents the Anglo-Catholic party in the Church of England. But those who hold it are not New Testament scholars, and most of them are simply not up to date in their reading on the subject. Thus the theory of the apostolic succession, like the theory of the verbal inspiration of the Bible, though still widely held by members of the Church of England, is not now regarded as compatible with a critical approach to the New Testament.

This conclusion is reinforced by the consideration that the theory has now been abandoned by well-informed Roman Catholic scholars and theologians also. The great merit of Raymond Brown's little book, published some five years ago, is that he honestly admits that we cannot trace deliberate succession from the Twelve to the first bishops.[3] (Raymond Brown is the leading theologian and biblical scholar in the Roman Catholic Church in America.) Karl Rahner (a distinguished German Jesuit theologian) commenting on *Lumen Gentium*, though not as explicit as Brown, obviously thinks that this document has claimed more than the evidence permits. He writes: 'First this transmission is proved (or merely asserted?) very briefly by appealing to the eschatological definiteness of the gospel', and he goes on to say that the validity of the proof is still a matter open to discussion.[4] We must understand how far-reaching are the consequences of this conclusion. Anglicans in the past have either leaned heavily on the theory of apostolic succession to supply them with a theology of the ministry, or been quite content to have no particular doctrine of the ministry at all. Neither of these positions is satisfactory; an attempt must be made to work out a theology of the ministry which does not depend on a doctrine of apostolic succession.

The development in the realm of practice has been the discovery that the catholic episcopate need not be confined to the Roman Catholic Church, the Orthodox Church, and the Anglican Communion. The breakthrough here came in 1947 when the Church of South India came into existence: this Church was made up of Anglicans, Methodists, Presbyterians, Congregationalists, and some elements from the tradition of the Reformed Church on the continent of Europe. Its first bishops were either themselves Anglican bishops or men who were at the inauguration of the Church consecrated to the episcopate by them. Of course all subsequent consecrations have been performed by bishops. In the scheme of union it was made clear that the non-episcopal churches joining the union, though they freely accepted episcopacy for the sake of union, were not bound to any particular interpretation of the meaning of episcopacy. This drew much Anglican criticism at the time; several distinguished Anglicans declared that episcopacy without any theory attached was quite useless. The history of CSI since 1947 has totally dissipated these fears and suspicions. Episcopacy is now an integral and much-appreciated feature of the Church. What is more, men who were brought up in non-episcopal traditions, when consecrated to the episcopate, have shown themselves not only well able to execute the office according to the best tradition of Anglicanism, but also able to find new and enriching values in the office itself. There have been occasions indeed when ex-Anglicans in the CSI have been startled and astonished to find bishops drawn from the Reformed tradition taking the episcopate a great deal more seriously than we have been accustomed to in Anglicanism—certainly more seriously than we have been used to taking bishops in the Church of England. They have assumed, quite rightly, that the bishop has a direct, spiritual, personal relationship to his flock that would be quite impossible in England, though it well may be more familiar in

other parts of the Anglican Communion. The Anglicans who
entered CSI believed that episcopacy was an institution which
would commend itself in use without demanding a theory to
accompany it as a *conditio sine qua non*. This has certainly
happened.

And now since 1970 we have in the Church of North India
another united Church which, as far as episcopacy is
concerned, has followed the example of CSI. But here the
range of Church traditions embraced in the union is much
wider, both historically and geographically. This Church is
already demonstrating that ex-Anglicans and ex-Baptists and
ex-Brethren can work harmoniously together in an episcopal
Church. The truth is that our various traditions, which we had
imagined to be incompatible, are very often complementary.
For example we found in CSI that the Anglican emphasis on
the great Church, as represented by the bishop in his diocese, is
not inconsistent with the Congregationalist emphasis on the
importance of the local congregation, but complementary to it.
Both can be included in the one Church and the Church is all
the richer for including both.

It is not surprising therefore that quite recently a group of
representative Anglicans and Roman Catholics have been able
to produce an agreed statement on the doctrine of the
ministry.[5] This statement does not cover all the points at issue
between the two Churches, but it covers some very important
areas. It does not specifically state that modern bishops are the
lineal successors of the apostles. It merely states 'at least by
the time of the Pastoral Epistles and 1 Peter, some ministerial
functions are discernible in a more exact form'. It admits that
'we have no evidence that "bishop" and "presbyter" were
appointed everywhere in the primitive period'. It expresses the
relation of the Christian priest to the eucharist thus 'it is right
that he who has oversight in the Church and is the focus of its
unity should preside at the celebration of the eucharist', and it
adds: 'So it is because the eucharist is central in the Church's
life that the essential nature of the Christian ministry, however
this may be expressed, is most clearly seen in its celebration'.
Ministers, it says, are 'representative of the whole Church in
the fulfilment of its priestly vocation of self-offering to God as

a living sacrifice'. The group who composed the statement add that this priesthood 'is not an extension of the common priesthood but belongs to another realm of the gifts of the Spirit'. Episcopal consecration, they say, ensures the historical continuity of this Church with the apostolic Church and of its bishop with the original apostolic ministry. They are well aware of the embarrassing fact that the Roman Catholic Church has already pronounced a negative verdict on Anglican orders by means of Leo XIII's Bull of 1896; but they suggest that the development of their thinking has 'put these issues in a new context'.

Some of this is open to criticism: one would like clarification of the phrase 'belongs to another realm of the gifts of the Spirit', and one cannot help thinking that the statement on continuity contains dangerous ambiguities. Does the group claim that modern bishops are connected with the original apostles by a continuous chain of laying-on of hands by bishops, or not? But we should not scrutinise this statement as if it were a legal document. We should be grateful for the degree of historical honesty about the origin of the ministry which the group has displayed; and we should rejoice that they have succeeded in so defining the relation of the priest to the eucharist that they ought at one and the same time to satisfy most reasonable Anglicans and allay the doubts which led Pope Leo XIII to pronounce his adverse verdict on Anglican orders.

By way of setting out our theology of the ministry we deal with four topics which should be considered first:

(A) VALIDITY

One of the problems which the Agreed Statement on the Ministry did not mention is the doctrine held officially by Roman Catholics and also by some Anglicans that ordination to the priesthood imprints on the soul an indelible character; that is the power to change the bread and wine into the body and blood of Christ by uttering the words of consecration in the eucharist. This is an extreme and over-explicit way of safeguarding a truth which the great majority of Christians would profess; the truth that orders cannot be removed and therefore need never be conferred twice on the same person. There is almost no Christian Church which, if it has conferred ministerial orders on a man and that man 'gives up his orders' for a period and then wishes to resume them, would actually reordain him. There is nothing strange in this, for the same thing applies to baptism, and indeed the Roman Catholic Church holds that baptism also confers an 'indelible character'. What Anglicans would rightly object to is the corollary that the character imprinted by ordination consists in the power to effect the change produced in eucharistic consecration. This narrows and individualises the eucharistic action in a most undesirable way, suggesting as it does that the priest has personal control over the eucharist independently of the worshipping congregation. It also carries the implication that, if the eucharist is celebrated in all good faith by someone who does not possess this power, 'nothing happens'; Christ refuses his presence to his people in the eucharist.

This entire approach to the ministry of the eucharist is traditionally expressed in terms of 'the validity of orders'. Pope Leo XIII, for example, would have held that Anglican orders were 'invalid' and that therefore Anglican priests were incapable of celebrating the eucharist effectively. Presumably when they attempted to do so, 'nothing happened'. Strict Anglo-Catholics would say the same thing (or used to say the same thing) about Free Church ministers. As long as the fierce inter-denominational rivalries which disgraced the Victorian Church were maintained, this attitude served well enough. Roman Catholics rejoiced to describe bishops of the Church of England as rebellious laymen, and some Anglicans were happy to pass on the compliment to Free Church ministers. But once let any element of charity creep in, once admit that those whose orders you disapprove do act in good faith and are really Christians in virtue of their baptism, and the entire theology of 'the validity of orders' begins to disintegrate. You have to admit, if you are a Roman Catholic, that, though the Anglican priest cannot validly consecrate the elements, Christ is not actually absent at Anglican eucharists. Next you have to define the difference between Christ's eucharistic presence at Catholic eucharists and his quasi-eucharistic presence at non-

Catholic eucharists. You end up with one of those purely verbal distinctions whose sole purpose is to satisfy scholastic theologians, bearing no relation whatever to empirical reality. You also find yourself casting Christ in a very peculiar rôle: he would like to be fully present at Anglican eucharists etc., but unfortunately, being bound by his own rules, he can only offer them a second-class presence.

Another, and more hopeful, way of getting round pronouncements about invalid orders, is to say that they only express a point of view; they do not say anything about reality or effectiveness. Thus when Leo XIII called Anglican orders 'utterly invalid and altogether void', he only meant that the Roman Catholic Church did not recognise them. They might all the same be quite adequate in fact. If Roman Catholics can persuade themselves that this is what Leo XIII really meant, Anglicans have no reason to complain.

Let us therefore drop all talk about validity and ask ourselves instead what it is that ordination confers. The answer, I believe, is authority to act in certain situations on behalf of the Church. This could equally be expressed as 'authority to act on behalf of Christ in the Church'. We have already observed that, if the Church is to exercise its authority at all, it must vest it in certain individuals. There are certain areas of the Church's activity where it cannot act by any other means. There is excommunication for example, an exercise of authority which, however rare in our post-Christendom situation in the West, is indispensable to the Church in certain situations. There is also the area of forgiveness of sins. The only justification for saying that a Christian priest can give absolution of sins to the penitent lies in the fact that the Church is concerned in the sins of its members. If one member suffers all the members suffer. Sin injures the corporate body, so the priest on behalf of Christ in the Church may reasonably be concerned with absolution. But we must repudiate the notion of the priest as the direct agent of Christ, so to speak issuing spiritual cheques which God is bound to honour, and equally the monstrous and tyrannical doctrine that the *only* means of forgiveness is by priestly absolution.

But the most obvious area in which the Church needs an

authorised representative is in the celebration of the eucharist. The celebrant should be a duly authorised minister here because the eucharist is the Church's rite and not a private devotion. Once allow indiscriminate lay celebration and the eucharist would soon become a private devotion like the Catholic's rosary or the Protestant's 'quiet time'. On this theory we need not be concerned whether any given eucharist is 'valid' or 'invalid', whether eucharistic grace is or is not available. Whenever Christ's people meet to celebrate the eucharist in good faith, Christ is present. We need not pass judgements on the value of any Christian eucharist.

This does not mean a doctrine of indiscriminate acceptance of everybody's orders. Order means Church authority. He who has the authority only of a tiny sect of his own making has very little authority. I can see no alternative to Oliver Quick's contention that in a state of divided Christendom all our orders are to some extent defective or irregular; we have found an echo of this doctrine in some modern Roman Catholic theologians.[6] Our aim should be, not to distinguish between valid and invalid ministries, but to try to unite the divided sections of the Church so that its ministry can have the greatest possible authority. Nor are we treating ministerial authority as if it could be taken away by the Church that gave it. It is Christ's authority in the Church. Ordination is therefore a sacramental act on the analogy of baptism and cannot be repeated. We must strive to avoid the two extremes of so qualifying ministerial authority as to make it ineffective on the one hand, and on the other of turning it into a personal prerogative to be exercised independently of the Church.

(B) THE THREEFOLD MINISTRY

The Church of the third, fourth, and fifth centuries conferred a whole series of orders below that of deacon, such as subdeacon, lector, exorcist, etc. They ceased to have any significance from about the seventh century onwards, but are preserved in a fossilised form in present Roman Catholic practice whereby these 'minor orders' are conferred all in one day on candidates for the priesthood. We can safely ignore them.

More relevant is the question of the diaconate. Catholics speak of 'the threefold ministry' of bishop, priest, and deacon, but in effect throughout Catholic Christendom the office of deacon has lost any individual significance it ever had and has become a preparatory stage for the priesthood. Some of the Free Churches use 'deacon' as an equivalent of 'elder'. A recent report prepared for the General Synod of the Church of England has concluded that we have no longer any use for the office of deacon, since everything that the deacon can do may be performed by laymen, and has proposed the abolition of the office. This seems unduly radical. On the contrary, with the growth and extension of purely lay ministries the time seems ripe for turning the diaconate into just that. In the last few years in particular the office of reader has come to the fore. Owing to the shortage of ordained clergy and the increasing difficulty of paying those there are, volunteer lay ministry, often prepared for by a period of study and training, is an obvious and commendable method of maintaining the pastoral, preaching, and to some extent liturgical activities of the Church. Why should not all such ministers, readers, Church Army captains, deaconesses, full-time women workers, be ordained to the diaconate? There would be no need whatever that deacons should wear a clerical collar or be addressed as 'Reverend'. It should be an unaffectedly lay order. Those who were destined for the priesthood need not become deacons first. There is need for such an order because, for example, not any and every lay person should be regarded as competent to preach at public worship. The requirement of a bishop's licence to preach is a necessary precaution. If therefore lay people should be licensed before preaching, why should this not apply to other activities, pastoral and liturgical? And if a whole series of laymen and women need licensing, would it not be better to incorporate them into the order of deacon? There seems to be an opportunity here for reviving an ancient institution and giving it new significance in the modern Church.

(c) THU ORDINATION OF WOMEN

This is a topic of burning interest in the Church of England today. It is not easy to present the issues calmly without incurring the accusation of partiality. All I can do is to sum up what seem to me to be the relevant arguments for and against. I omit some often-used arguments which I regard as irrelevant; for example any arguments drawn from the nature of the Old Testament priesthood; the argument which says 'what would the Roman Catholics say if we ordained women to the priesthood?'; or the contemptuous argument which runs 'let the women have the priesthood if they want it'.

Arguments in favour of ordination of women to the priesthood

1. A number of devout, well-educated and well-balanced women claim that they have a call to the priesthood. Many of them have already served in full-time pastoral ministry with marked success. It seems dogmatic and arrogant to say to them: 'We know that the Holy Spirit has not called you to this office.'

2. During the last seventy years in the West women have sought and obtained admission to all other professions, notably that of medicine, law, the highest ranks of the Civil Service, including diplomacy, and education, including the highest posts in the universities. They have shown that they are quite capable of executing these offices effectively. The arguments used in the past by doctors, lawyers etc. in an effort to exclude them bear a remarkable resemblance to some of those now being used against the ordination of women. This is an argument from analogy, but it is no less cogent for that.

3. It is difficult to find weighty theological objections to their ordination. Moreover Gal. 3.28 would seem to give a strong argument in favour: 'There is neither Jew nor Greek, there is neither slave nor free, there is neither male nor female, for you are all one in Christ Jesus.' All the other distinctions have been transcended as far as the ministry is concerned: why not this one?

4. Ever since the Reformation the status of women in the Church of England has been unnaturally depressed, yet they have never ceased to take a share in the Church's pastoral ministry. In the past too much of this has fallen to the lot of clergy wives, whose devoted service has perhaps masked the fact that the question of the ministry of women has not hitherto

been squarely faced by the Church of England. It is unjust that highly qualified women should still be offered nothing more than subordinate office in the Church.

5. The main reason why women were not ordained in previous centuries has been a sociological one: woman's status in society made it inconceivable. In the West this is no longer the case. Women can, and do, have a career of their own both before and after bearing and rearing children.

Arguments against the ordination of women to the priesthood

1. There is no precedent in catholic tradition. Only heretics, or (in our day) Protestants have ordained women to the ministry. The Church of England should not on her own take a step which breaks so long a tradition. (As a matter of fact we should note that already within the Anglican Communion a woman has been canonically ordained to the priesthood both in Kenya and in Hong Kong.)

2. There is no scriptural warrant for it. St Paul would undoubtedly have disapproved of it; see 1 Cor. 11.2–16; 14.33–6; 1 Tim. 2.11–15.

3. The incarnation of God was through a male, Jesus Christ: the priest represents Christ and therefore must be (or ought to be) a male.

4. The ministry was given to us in its present form by Christ. We are not entitled to change it so drastically as to permit women to enter the priesthood.

5. We speak of God as Father on the authority of our Lord himself. The Church is a family of which God is the Father. When the family meets round the Lord's table, he who presides should be a male in order to preserve this essential imagery. The New Testament does attribute authority in the family to the father.

We must comment on some of these arguments. It is quite true that Paul would not have approved of a woman-priest (had he known of such an office). But we know why: it is because he understands the story of Eve being taken out of Adam's side literally (Gen. 2.20–24). This is an argument which would carry weight with few educated Christians in the West today.

Besides it proves too much: Paul would have disapproved quite as much of women judges, hospital consultants, and university professors.[7] Again the argument drawn from the nature of the incarnation assumes that the priest is a direct representative of Christ. But we have argued that his priesthood comes through the Church, which is made up of men and women. Similarly the argument based on the unchangeable nature of the ministry assumes that the ministry was given to the Church in its present form (or in any form) by Christ. This is not borne out by the evidence.

I personally would conclude that there is no really cogent argument against the ordination of women and that the Church of England ought to permit it. The more courageous course is usually the right one. But let us not forget that women are not just substitute men; if they are ordained to the priesthood, they will exercise their ministry in a different style to the way men do it. This will be beneficial to the Church, since the differences between the sexes is ordained by God for our good.

(D) THE POSITION OF THE CLERGY IN SOCIETY

A number of social developments have combined to make the full-time paid clergyman today in the West feel that his status is threatened; first, the rise of the welfare state has meant that very many of the social activities which he formerly carried out have been taken over by the state. Too often he sees the professional social worker as his successful rival. Again, the wide extension of secondary education has in many cases deprived him of his position of natural leadership as one of the few educated persons in the community. More than this, laity (including a large number of women) are now receiving a university education in theology. The parish priest must sometimes face a situation in which some members of his congregation are better qualified in theology than he is himself. The democratic and egalitarian *Zeitgeist* makes it more difficult for him to assert an authority which is fundamentally voluntary and spiritual and is enforced by none of the economic and professional sanctions enjoyed by social workers, doctors, and teachers. Finally, growing inflation threatens his livelihood more immediately than it does that of those who are paid by the state. His social status has slumped sharply during the last thirty years.

These developments are not by any means disastrous or disadvantageous to the ministry. The social worker is certainly better paid and sometimes assumes a position of superiority to the parish priest (though more often perhaps there is admirable co-operation). But the priest at least is free from the stigma of being something laid on by the state to which the citizen has a natural right. He is more likely to be accepted as someone whose service is authentic and altruistic than is the social worker, despite the undoubted dedication and altruism of many social workers. Experience proves that the existence of more lay responsibility in the Church and better qualified lay people does not necessarily lower the status of the priest. On the contrary he is all the more appreciated for what he can do. The fact that priestly authority is now seen to be voluntary and spiritual, and is not enforced by the sanction of either state or society, is a gain not a loss. This is how God intends it to be. This is how it was in the Church of St Paul's day. As for the question of livelihood, here is a source of real hardship nobly borne by most clergy. There will certainly in the future have to be a wide extension of the voluntary, part-time or spare-time priesthood. There is no theological objection to this whatever. Once more, it is a return to the conditions of the primitive Church. It may be that all this social change is in fact 'God's left hand'. He is bringing us back to the condition in which he wills that we should serve him best.

How then shall we define the ordained ministry? We must be clear about what can, and what cannot, be claimed on its behalf. We cannot claim that our Lord instituted the ordained ministry, nor even that he planned it or intended it. Since it is not dominical in origin (unlike the two sacraments), it must have its origin in the Church. This is not a second-best theology, but one which is entirely consonant with the witness of the New Testament. But it follows that we must not so define the ministry as to make it independent of the Church, still less so as to place the Church entirely in the hands of the ministry. This has happened in history, with disastrous consequences. One of the worst of mediaeval corruptions was the way in which government, discipline, and doctrine had been entirely monopolised by the clerical hierarchy, so that in theory at least no layman had any right to question any ecclesiastical decision. Painful and unhappy though the consequences of the Reformation were for the Church in the West, it did at least break the stranglehold which the clerical order was exercising over the Church; and for that we should be thankful. Not that the Churches of the Reformation can boast today of having freed themselves from that excessive clericalisation which is a legacy of the Middle Ages. On the contrary, the briefest study of the quotation from William Temple's presidential address which we cited on p. 97 will show how completely he is still under the conviction that the ministry is independent of the Church. If we follow his argument as set out there, we must conclude that, had Archbishop Temple decided on his own initiative to ordain men to the priesthood in his back drawing-room without consulting the Church, the Church of England would have been compelled to accept them as true priests. He claims that his ordinations (note the personal emphasis) are carried out in the Church, but there does not seem to be any theological reason, on his assumptions, why the Church should be concerned at all. If so high-minded, saintly, and learned a man as William Temple could give utterance to such a theology of the ministry amid universal applause from the Church, how far gone we must be in a deeply clericalised and unscriptural doctrine of ministry! Apostolic succession as a credible account of the origin of the ministry is dead, but its ghost still exercises a vast influence in the Church of England.

If therefore our doctrine of the ministry requires that the ministry be integrally related to the Church, we must understand clearly what we mean by the laity. The theology of the laity is a subject which has only comparatively recently formed a topic of study among theologians. In the past the laity has either been totally subordinated to the clergy, or regarded as the genuine article as contrasted with the ministers who are paid Christians. The two extremes are beautifully delineated in two quotations which we shall reproduce. The first is from an encyclical *Vehementer* of Pope Pius X (reigned

1903–14): 'In the pastoral body alone resides the right and authority necessary to advance and direct all the members towards the end of the society. The multitude has no other right than to let itself be led and to follow its shepherds as an obedient flock.' The other quotation is a brilliant quip by T. W. Manson. He claims that, according to some Free Church Christians 'a minister is a layman who has lost his amateur status'.[8]

The ordained ministry represents the Church; not some transcendental Church which can therefore never demand an account from its ministers, but the empirical, visible Church in which they serve. If this Church, despite all its sins, can yet be described as the body of Christ in the Pauline sense, the ministry has no right to look beyond it to some more holy or more authoritative body to which it is (in Christ) responsible. From this it follows that the whole Church, not just the ordained part of it, has responsibility for the Church's life and activity in the world. Hence the laity not only may be, but ought to be, associated with the clergy in all matters of faith, discipline, and morals. The government of the Church ought not to be wholly in the hands of clerics; laity ought to be associated with clergy here also. Naturally no-one can lay down a blueprint for *how* this is to be done. Methods will differ with different cultures and different periods. The movement to give the laity a bigger share in the government of the Church of England was largely inspired by the triumph of democracy in the West, with the natural result that we tend to want to give the Church a modern democratic system of government. This is not necessarily the best way, but it is better than the old method of episcopal autocracy tempered by government interference and the parson's freehold.

As a matter of fact this ideal of ministerial, representative priesthood, rather than vicarious, autocratic priesthood, has already been outlined in what is the classic book on the theology of the ministry as far as Anglicans are concerned, R. C. Moberly's *Ministerial Priesthood*.[9] Moberly was writing only a few years after Leo XIII's Bull condemning Anglican orders and no doubt this is the main reason why he wrote when he did. But fortunately for us Moberly does not confine himself to anti-Roman polemic or to outdated efforts to prove the apostolic succession. He also outlines an admirable theology of the ministry. He freely concedes that the priesthood of the ministry comes from the priesthood of Christ through the priesthood of the whole Church. Christian priesthood is therefore, he says, representative or ministerial, not vicarious. By a 'vicarious' priesthood he means one in which the priest is vicar for the Church, acts in its place, is its surrogate or substitute. He believed that the Roman Catholic theology of his day presented a picture of a vicarious priesthood. The priesthood of the ordained ministry is not identical with the priesthood of all Christians, but it springs from it and is derived from it. The minister's priesthood is not different in kind from that which belongs corporately to all Christians. The ordained priesthood is an instrument and organ of the corporate priesthood of the Church conferred in baptism.

All Christian priesthood springs from Christ's priesthood. But the very centre of Christ's priesthood consists in his self giving on behalf of men. The key text is Mark 10.45: 'For the Son of man also came not to be served but to serve, and to give his life as a ransom for many.' Christian priesthood therefore must be basically this sort of priesthood, one expressed in service and self-giving. Moberly does not exclude the eucharistic element in priesthood, but he wishes to keep it in its place. In the Roman Catholic system of his day, the eucharistic element had been so moved to the centre as to put the pastoral element nearer the periphery. His book is an effort to redress the balance.

But Moberly also insists that the Church does possess divine authority and should be enabled to exercise it. This is something of which we in the Church of England need reminding. For various social and historical reasons we have allowed the concept of discipline and authority in the Church to fall into the background. Perhaps the establishment of the General Synod as the ultimate authority in the Church of England (with all its faults) may serve to bring us back to a true sense of authority. But imagine the indignation that would be caused in the mind of the average parish priest if, for example, a diocesan bishop attempted to tell his clergy in any detail what they ought, and what they ought not, to teach and preach! Yet if the Church does have authority, and if that authority is exercised by means of the ordained ministry, this is one of the most obvious areas in which one might expect to see it manifested. It may be, as we have suggested when considering Paul's doctrine of the ministry, that churchly authority can only be ultimately exercised not coercively but in terms of suffering. This has certainly been the case in many instances among the Churches in Eastern Europe and Russia under hostile Communist régimes. The authorities of the Church, unable to exercise their authority directly because of persecution or harassment, have had to vindicate their authority by suffering or even martyrdom. It has certainly proved surprisingly effective as far as concerns the survival of the Church under conditions of discrimination and difficulty.

We have in fact defined the ministry in terms of the Church, and not the Church in terms of the ministry. This is closer to Cyprian's ideal and farther away from that of Western Catholicism.[10] It is also much closer to what we find in the New Testament, where the Church is central and the ministry as such peripheral or subordinate to the Church. This understanding of ministry should mean that Anglicans can afford to take a much more relaxed approach to questions of reunion than we have in the past. Not that we can, or should, renounce episcopacy in our negotiations with other Churches. But we do not need to demand as a condition of reunion that all non-Anglican ministers must receive some sort of episcopal commission. Professor G. W. H. Lampe in a recent article has pointed out the significance of what he calls 'the Limuru Principle'.[11] This is the suggestion, made at the first meeting of the Anglican Consultative Council in Limuru in 1971, that what matters for Anglicans is not necessarily that all ministers under the jurisdiction of the diocesan bishop should have been episcopally ordained. It is enough, at the outset at least, that they all 'share with him in one common liturgical life and act under his pastoral leadership'. If this could be accepted as a general rule in our negotiations for reunion with other Churches, much misunderstanding and difficulty would be avoided without the sacrifice of theological principle.

The modern Anglican has to offer a reasoned defence for episcopacy. He cannot take it for granted. He should not claim that it was instituted by our Lord, or that it exists *iure divino*, or that it is necessary for the very existence of the Church (all claims that Anglicans have made in the past). This does not mean that it cannot be defended.

The defence should rest, I believe, on three points. The first is tradition: episcopacy has existed as the form of Church order since very early in the second century. Only since the Reformation have there been Churches without it. It is therefore older than the oldest creeds and liturgies. Apart from the celebration of the sacraments itself, which has been continuous since the time of the incarnation, it is the oldest of the Church's institutions. This is not a negative argument from tradition, like that employed in the case against the ordination of women, but a positive one. Like all the Church's institutions episcopacy is not invulnerable to corruption, and it had fallen into considerable corruption by the time of the Reformation. But the same could be said of the eucharist.

Secondly, episcopacy has a positive theological significance as well. One of the features which distinguishes Christianity (as well as Judaism and Islam) from the great Eastern religions is its claim that God is personal. Indeed in Christianity as compared with Judaism and Islam this claim is emphasised, because Christians believe that God has supremely manifested and communicated himself to men in a person. Now episcopacy, when rightly exercised (as is not always the case in the Church of England), is a personal ministry. The bishop should have a personal, spiritual relationship to his clergy, and if possible to the laity of his diocese also, not a purely administrative, bureaucratic one. The bishop in person represents the great Church to his diocese, and his own local Church to the greater Church. This, when rightly done, is best done by a person. There can be a true personal episcopal functioning. Perhaps the best place to see this is in Anglican Churches outside England. We have certainly seen this in the Church of South India: Christians, who previously had no experience of episcopal oversight, have recognised the personal significance of the bishop. He is *their* father-in-God.

Thirdly, there is a value in historic succession. Professor Torrance, a distinguished theologian of the Church of Scotland, has written: 'Validity also refers to the responsible transmission of authorization from generation to generation, attesting the obedience of the Church in all its ordinations to the apostolic teaching and ordinances.'[12] We might say that historic succession is the sign, but not the sacrament, of the continuity of the Church in time. It is not the sacrament, because it does not effect the continuity. The Church itself is the sacrament of continuity. But the sign is a valuable sign and may not be lightly disregarded.

One warning should be uttered about episcopacy: Anglicans should defend *diocesan* episcopacy. Other sorts of bishops, such as suffragans, auxiliary bishops, or coadjutor bishops, it is, I believe, impossible to defend on any of the three grounds we have just set out. They are the marks of a bureaucratic Church that is in danger of losing the personal character of episcopacy. It is much to be hoped that the Church of England will cease to make use of them. Still more objectionable is the Roman Catholic habit of conferring the episcopate on a man purely as a mark of honour. It reminds one too much of what Jesus said was the custom of the Gentiles: 'You know that those who are supposed to rule over the Gentiles lord it over them, and their great men exercise authority over them. But it shall not be so among you' (Mark 10.42–3). Others have suggested that the Church of England might experiment with groups or colleges of bishops exercising joint jurisdiction within a given area. This looks like just one more effort to preserve huge dioceses, too large for the bishop to maintain personal touch with his people. If we want a college, we have it in the bishop with his fellow-presbyters.

We must not forget that mere episcopacy is not only rejected by Free Churchmen, but also by Roman Catholics, who contend that it is incomplete and indeed illegitimate without the papacy. The scriptural proofs whereby Roman Catholic scholars have attempted in the past to prove the divine right of the bishop of Rome to the obedience of all Christians need not be discussed by us. They are no better founded than the traditional proofs for the apostolic succession and require even more acts of faith to make up the gaps in the historical evidence. It is indeed doubtful whether modern Roman Catholic scholars would seek to present them today as they have been presented in the past. The full papal claims however are still maintained by the contemporary pope, Paul VI, despite his undeniable desire for ecumenical *rapprochement*. When they are made, Anglicans must still reject them.

There are some signs that some modern Roman Catholic theologians are prepared to look at this most controversial topic in a new light. Many of them would admit that the papal office has not been presented to those outside the Roman Catholic Church in a very attractive light. All the emphasis has been on power and jurisdiction. As Hans Küng says, the task of the Roman Catholic Church is to make the Petrine office credible once more: 'The Petrine office in the last resort should be concerned not with its righteousness, authority, and power, but with ministering to the brethren.'[13] Even a more representative theologian such as Karl Rahner has pointed out that strictly speaking the Pope alone does not wield the supreme power in the Roman Catholic Church, but 'the college constituted under the Pope as its primatial head'.[14]

Another Roman Catholic theologian has written: 'it could be that for the Protestant what stands in the way of belief in the Petrine office—which *is* based on the Bible—is the *form* which that office currently assumes'.[15] If so, it is appropriate that we end this book with a brief review of the advantages which a reformed papacy could bring to a united Church. It would provide us with a supranational figure of great moral authority, who could sometimes exercise wholesome restraint over Churches experiencing pressure from extreme nationalism. It could be a focus of unity for the whole Church and a symbol of that unity hallowed by centuries of tradition. It could act as a clearing house for international Christianity, bringing together the riches of local Christianity from all over the world for the benefit of the whole Church. Anglicans are not irrevocably committed to oppose the papacy in any form. What we rejected in the sixteenth century was the *tyranny* of the bishop of Rome. But our last word must be that all these advantages would be purchased at too high a price if we were to accept them on the terms still officially proposed.

Nevertheless in the sphere of the doctrine of the ministry very great progress has been made during the last few years in the way of mutual understanding among Christians of varying traditions. Never since the Reformation has there been a brighter hope for those who seek by a deeper understanding of the meaning of the ministry to heal the divisions of the Christian Church.

Notes

CHAPTER 1

[1] See Paul Minear, *Images of the Church in the New Testament* (London, 1961).
[2] E. Schweizer sets out his views in the article on *sōma* in the *Theological Dictionary of the New Testament* (Eng. trans., vol. VII, Michigan, 1971). See also E. Schweizer, *The Church as the Body of Christ* (London, 1966).
[3] See A. M. Ramsey, *The Gospel and the Catholic Church* (2nd edn, London, 1955), p. 35.
[4] See R. Newton Flew, ed., *The Nature of the Church* (London, 1952), p. 50.
[5] See J. Feine's essay in *Commentary on the Documents of Vatican II* (ed. H. Vorgrimler), vol. II, p. 74 (Eng. trans. London, 1968 of German edn of 1967).

CHAPTER 2

[1] An English translation of these two documents can be found in W. M. Abbot, ed., *The Documents of Vatican II* (London, 1965).
[2] See B. Leeming, *The Vatican Council and Christian Unity* (London, 1966), p. 84.
[3] See H. Küng, *Infallible?* (Eng. trans., London, 1971 of German edn, 1970).
[4] See J. N. Ward, *Five for Sorrow, Ten for Joy* (london, 1971).
[5] See H. Küng, *Structures of the Church* (Eng. trans., London, 1964), p. 145.
[6] See his book *The Christian Sacraments* (2nd edn, London, 1932).
[7] See *Commentary on the Documents of Vatican II*, vol. II, pp. 92–3.

CHAPTER 3

[1] See M. Werner, *The Formation of Christian Dogma* (Eng. trans., London, 1957).
[2] See D. M. Baillie, *The Theology of the Sacraments* (London, 1957), p. 51.

[3] See K. Rahner, *Theological Investigations 4* (Eng. trans., London, 1960 of German edn, 1960), p. 274.

[4] *Ibid.*, p. 254.

[5] D. M. Baillie, *op. cit.*, p. 60.

[6] See G. Wainwright, *Christian Initiation* (London, 1969), p. 24.

[7] See for example R. R. Osborn, *Forbid Them Not* (London, 1972).

[8] See George Every, *The Baptismal Sacrifice* (London, 1959), p. 94.

CHAPTER 4

[1] Eng. trans., Oxford, 1955 of German edn of 1949 (new edn, London, 1966 of German 4th edn of 1964).

[2] H. Lietzmann, *Mass and Lord's Supper* (Eng. trans., London, 1934).

[3] See A. R. C. Leaney, 'What Was the Lord's Supper?' in *Theology*, Feb. 1967, p. 55.

[4] These conclusions owe much to the solution outlined by Oscar Cullmann; see his book *Early Christian Worship* (Eng. trans., London, 1953) and also O. Cullmann and F. L. Leenhardt, *Essays in the Lord's Supper* (Eng. trans., London, 1958).

[5] *Dialogue with Trypho*, 116.

[6] Gregory Dix, *The Shape of the Liturgy* (London, 1945), p. 158. I have slightly abbreviated the summary.

[7] See *The Baptismal Sacrifice*, p. 91.

[8] *Ibid.*, p. 106.

[9] See A. C. Clark, ed., *Modern Eucharistic Agreement* (London, 1973), p. 27.

[10] *Ibid.*, p. 38.

[11] See E. Schillebeeckx, *The Eucharist* (Eng. trans., London, 1968 of Dutch edn of 1967), p. 41.

[12] For all these references see *op. cit.*, pp. 77–8, 101, 110, 137, 139, 141, 150.

[13] For these references see Karl Rahner, *Theological Investigations 4* (Eng. trans., London, 1960 of German edn of 1960), pp. 285, 298f., 302, 319.

[14] See *Agreed Statements on Eucharist and Ministry*, pp. 28, 29, 31.

[15] *Ibid.*, pp. 40, 43, 44.

[16] Compare the description given by the *Group of Les Dombes*: 'a joyful anticipation of the heavenly banquet' (*Agreed Statements on Eucharist and Ministry*, p. 62).

[17] See D. M. Baillie, *The Theology of the Sacraments* (London, 1957), p. 123.

CHAPTER 5

[1] This is not inconsistent with the view that the two evangelists meant it to apply to the position of the ministry in the Church of their day.

[2] I do not regard the Pastoral Epistles as Pauline and deal with them separately later.

[3] I have deliberately followed the *NEB* here rather than the *RSV* because I believe the *NEB* renders the sense more correctly.

[4] The quotation is taken from H. Bettenson, *Documents of the Christian Church* (London, 1943), p. 89.

[5] The quotation is from J. H. Bernard in his article, 'The Cyprianic Doctrine of the Ministry', in *Essays on the History of the Early Church and Ministry*, ed. H. B. Swete (London, 1918), p. 244.

[6] I have ventured to paraphrase Cyprian's extremely terse Latin: 'Episcopatus unus est, cuius a singulis in solidum pars tenetur'.

[7] Quoted from William Temple's presidential address to Convocation, May 1943.

[8] Quoted from Bettenson, *op. cit.*, p. 382.

CHAPTER 6

[1] See W. M. Abbott, *op. cit.*, p. 37.

[2] London, 1946; revised edn, A. Farrer (London, 1957).

[3] Raymond Brown, *Priest and Bishop: Biblical Reflections* (London, 1970).

[4] See H. Vorgrimler, *op. cit.*, p. 90.

[5] H. R. McAdoo and A. C. Clark, eds, *Ministry and Ordination* (London, 1973).

[6] For example, J. Feine's statement: 'as long as the divisions of the Church endure, it is not possible to bring into being the fullness of catholicity proper to the Church'; Vorgrimler, *op. cit.*, vol. II, p. 93.

[7] Some of the biblical evidence cited here is also suspect: textual evidence suggests that 1 Cor. 14.34–5 may not have been an original part of the Epistle. Some scholars believe that these verses were inserted by the author of the Pastorals. Likewise of course 1 Tim. 2.11–15 will only have Pauline authority in the eyes of those who believe that Paul wrote the Pastorals; probably a diminishing group.

[8] See T. W. Manson, *Ministry and Priesthood, Christ's and Ours* (London, 1958), p. 41.

[9] Originally issued in 1897 (London); it has been reprinted with a modern introduction by SPCK (London, 1969).

[10] It is also possibly closer to the position of the Orthodox Church. Though Orthodox Christians are absolutely inflexible on the necessity of the episcopate, they have a great regard for the importance of the sense of the whole Church, laity included; and they have a principle of 'economy' whereby they can on occasion accept anomalies for the sake of some overriding benefit.

[11] See 'The "Limuru Principle" and Church Unity', in *The Churchman*, Jan.–March 1974, p. 25.

[12] T. F. Torrance, *Conflict and Agreement in the Church*, vol. 2 (London, 1960), p. 49.

[13] H. Küng, *Structures of the Church* (Eng. trans., London, 1964), pp. 203–4.

[14] See Vorgrimler, *op. cit.*, p. 203.

[15] See R. Adolfs, *The Church is Different* (Eng. trans., London, 1966 of Dutch edn of 1964), p. 117.

Suggestions for further reading

THE CHURCH

The Vatican II Documents and a very illuminating commentary on them by leading Roman Catholic theologians can be found in:

W. M. Abbot, ed., *The Documents of Vatican II* (London, 1956).
H. Vorgrimler, ed., *Commentary on the Documents of Vatican II* (2 vols., London, 1968).

For the Church in the New Testament, read:

Paul Minear, *Images of the Church in the New Testament* (London, 1961).
E. Schweizer, *The Church as the Body of Christ* (London, 1966).

For the doctrine of the Church:

R. Newton Flew, *The Nature of the Church* (London, 1952). This gives statements from theologians representative of various traditions. It is Pre-Vatican II.
H. Küng, *Structures of the Church* (London, 1964).
——, *The Church* (London, 1967).
——, *Infallible?* (London, 1970).
A somewhat 'way out' Roman Catholic theologian, but well worth listening to on this topic.

SACRAMENTS

D. M. Baillie, *The Theology of the Sacraments* (London, 1957). A first-class Scottish theologian writes on both sacraments.
Karl Rahner, *Theological Investigations 4* (London, 1960). A very good discussion of sacraments in general and the eucharist in particular.
George Every, *The Baptismal Sacrifice*; an acute presentation of baptism by an Anglican monk who has recently joined the Church of Rome.

E. C. WHITAKER, *Documents of the Baptismal Liturgy* (2nd edn., London, 1970). Useful historical information about the development of baptism.

G. WAINWRIGHT, *Christian Initiation* (London, 1969). A learned Methodist theologian puts the issues concerning baptism very clearly.

R. R. OSBORN, *Forbid them Not* (London, 1972). An eloquent plea for unrestricted infant baptism.

A. GILMORE, ed., *Christian Baptism* (London, 1959). A learned and restrained presentation of the case against paedo-baptism by a group of Baptist scholars.

J. D. C. FISHER, *Christian Initiation: Baptism in the Mediaeval West* (London, 1965).

M. PERRY, ed., *Crisis for Confirmation* (London, 1967).
These last two books help one to understand the predicament of the Church of England over baptism and confirmation.

H. LIETZMANN, *Mass and Lord's Supper* (London, 1934).

J. JEREMIAS, *The Eucharistic Words of Jesus* (London, 1955).

O. CULLMANN, *Early Christian Worship* (London, 1953).
These last three books explore the New Testament evidence about the eucharist.

O. CULLMANN and F. L. LEENHARDT, *Essays in the Lord's Supper* (London, 1958). An admirable study by two theologians of the Swiss Reformed tradition.

E. SCHILLEBEECKX, *The Eucharist* (London, 1968). A book by a Roman Catholic theologian who appreciates the difficulties of the traditional account of the doctrine of transubstantiation.

GREGORY DIX, *The Shape of the Liturgy* (London, 1945). A stimulating and original study of the early eucharist by an Anglican monk who wrote like an angel.

A. C. CLARK, *Modern Eucharistic Agreement* (London, 1973). Gives the text of several important documents.

MINISTRY

E. SCHWEIZER, *Church Order in the New Testament* (London, 1961). A review of the biblical evidence by a first-class biblical scholar.

R. C. MOBERLY, *Ministerial Priesthood* (new edn, London, 1969). The best Anglican statement of the doctrine of ministry.

K. KIRK, *The Apostolic Ministry* (new edn, London, 1946). The best case that can be made on historical grounds for the doctrine of apostolic succession.

T. W. MANSON, *Ministry and Priesthood, Christ's and Ours* (London, 1958). An excellent exposition from the high church Reformed point of view.

A. T. HANSON, *The Pioneer Ministry* (London, 1961). An exposition in detail of the view of the New Testament ministry outlined here.

H. R. MCADOO and A. C. CLARK, *Ministry and Ordination* (London, 1973). Contains the agreed Anglican–Roman Catholic statement on ordination.

RAYMOND BROWN, *Priest and Bishop: Biblical Reflections* (London, 1970). A very honest review of the New Testament evidence by a modern Roman Catholic scholar.

R. P. C. HANSON, *Groundwork for Unity* (London, 1971). 'Plain facts about Christian unity' set forth by a modern Anglican theologian.

Index of Biblical References

General Index